THERE'S A ROAD TO EVERYWHERE EXCEPT WHERE YOU CAME FROM

A MEMOIR BY
BRYAN CHARLES

 **OPEN CITY BOOKS**

New York

An excerpt of this book previously appeared in *Open City*.

Printed in the United States of America
Published simultaneously in Canada

Book and cover design by Nick Stone

Library of Congress Control Number: 2010935516

ISBN-13: 978-1-890447-57-1

OPEN CITY BOOKS
270 Lafayette Street
New York, NY 10012
www.opencity.org

10 11 12 13 14 15   10 9 8 7 6 5 4 3 2 1

For

Paul Bayer

Trish Chappell

Karla Wozniak

Author's Note

This book begins on 10/1/98 and ends on 1/14/02. It was written with the aid of contemporaneous personal journals. Many names have been changed. Dialogue was written as closely as I could remember it and in some cases consists of composite conversations. Chronology was rendered as close to the actual sequence of events as I could recall.

something
is working toward you
right now, and
I mean you
and nobody but
you.

—Charles Bukowski

The Condition

I arrived in New York after a twenty-five-hour train ride carrying two bags of clothes and a banker's box full of papers. Erin met me at Penn Station and led me through the crush of people and out to the street. We got in a cab and headed uptown. The cab cut through traffic going what felt like eighty miles an hour. Blocks blurred by. Neighborhoods changed. She lived in a sublet on the Upper West Side. We pulled off on a pretty street lined with trees and old brownstones. Inside I called my parents and told them I'd arrived safely. I cleaned myself up a bit and Erin took me to get dinner—two slices at Famous Original Ray's.

Back at the apartment we watched TV. I'd barely slept on the train and faded quickly. We got into bed. For a moment I was on one side and Erin was on the other. Then we slid over into each other's arms. She ran a hand up my back and gripped the back of my neck.

—We're gonna kiss now, she said.

The next day we met Craig at a diner in Midtown for lunch. He and Erin caught up a bit. They talked about city life.

We finished eating and walked to Craig's office, a minimalist space with bare concrete walls and desks out in the open on a bare concrete floor with a few offices to the side. Everyone wore street clothes and worked on Macs. They sat low in their seats staring blankly at big monitors, clicking at boxes and shapes on the screen. Craig started writing out directions to the place. I tried to follow what he was saying but grew confused. I admitted I was scared to take the subway alone. It was decided I'd come back after he got out of work and we'd go into Brooklyn together.

I returned that evening around six and stood on a corner in Times Square loaded down with my bags, clutching the banker's box. Hundreds of people streamed past me and their faces all blurred. I began to feel dizzy. I was relieved to see Craig. He grabbed one of my bags. We went into the subway.

It was a railroad apartment in Greenpoint consisting of a large kitchen, a living room, and two open back rooms with no wall or even a sheet between them. The floors of the living room and middle room were covered with worn brown carpet. The floor in the back room was covered with old salmon-colored carpet and there was a pink sponged paint pattern on a jutting section of the wall. In the living room was a futon couch, a small blue chair, and a large closet with plastic doors on runners. Inside the closet a TV sat on two Huber Bock beer boxes, clothes hanging on either side of it. Paul had rigged an antennae and pinned it up with one of his old Kmart nametags. On the wall was an inflatable bull's eye with velcro strips, three or four balls stuck to the velcro. On the floor under the bull's eye was a plastic cactus in a plastic pot with fake scrub brush. The lower half of the kitchen walls were wood-paneled. Over the sink were copper-colored tiles with images of mushrooms stamped on them. Paul had made a counter from a piece of wood and a large cardboard box. He'd glued the wood to the top of the box and covered the whole thing with an old blue sheet. On the counter next to a coffee maker was a magazine photo of a croissant, steaming coffee, fruit, and juice. The photo had been placed in a gold plastic frame. There was no sink in the tiny bathroom.

Craig slept in the middle room on a twin mattress on the floor. Also in the room were his stereo, some records, his desk and computer. Ten feet away on the floor under one of two windows was a full-size mattress. It belonged to Paul but he was away till November working a temp-labor gig at a nuclear power plant and so it was temporarily mine. I fell asleep fully clothed that first night under an open window, listening to cars pass on the street three floors below.

Rent was nine hundred dollars split three ways. I wrote Craig a check for October's rent, which left me with roughly twelve hundred bucks. I figured this would carry me a while. I decided to get to know the city rather than look for a job right away. Every day I'd take the train to Manhattan and walk for hours. Often I'd stop and see Erin at work. She worked at a comedy club in the west twenties. She sat at a desk in a basement office, reading newspapers, smoking, and answering the phone. The club was on its last legs. The phone didn't ring much. We'd sit for a long time shooting the breeze. There was a *New York Post* editorial cartoon on the wall—a deranged Bill Clinton on St. Patrick's Day saying *Where is this Erin with no bra?*

I'd tell her what I'd seen and done that day. Erin would recommend things to add to my list. I went to Harlem, Times Square, Central Park. I went to a taping of the Ricki Lake show. I went to an appearance by Jennifer Love Hewitt at an HMV store in Midtown. I had a thing for JLH, dug *I Know What You Did Last Summer.*

I went to the top of the Empire State building and looked out at the city. It was a clear day and I could see to the end of the island. This may have been the first time I saw the World Trade Center in person. I went down there a few days later. I stood on the plaza between the two towers, tilted my head, and looked straight up. A feeling of vertigo came over me. I almost fell down.

A similar sensation began to afflict me on my city walks generally, an odd dislocation, as if my head were a balloon floating twenty feet in the air, connected to my body by a thin string. This balloon head had camera eyes that would record the action and play it back to me. I seemed not to be experiencing events firsthand. This feeling could last an hour or more. I told Paul about it one night over the phone. He said he knew the feeling and described a few times it had happened to him. We gave it a name: the Condition.

Erin took me to a comedy show at the Roseland Ballroom. One of the people on the bill was her ex-boyfriend Stephen. I'd heard a lot about Stephen over the last couple years. Erin had moved to New York with him in the late summer of '96, just a few months after she and I split up. She always said she thought Stephen and I would get along. I didn't doubt her exactly but felt threatened by Stephen, by their history together and now his success. Others had told me how great he was—talented, funny, destined to hit it big. I was prepared to dislike him on principle.

We watched his set and had a beer with him later. It was clear within seconds I couldn't hate him, he truly was a good guy. We rapped about Kalamazoo and some of our mutual friends. We rapped about the Yankees and Chuck Knoblauch's boneheaded move in the ALCS a couple weeks ago, arguing with the umpire while the ball was still in play as Indians base runners advanced and a run scored. Stephen had been at the game.

After the show we stood on Fifty-second Street saying goodbye. I got an odd feeling as we walked away from him. I almost felt sort of sad.

I turned to Erin on the subway.

—Do you think Stephen still likes you?

—Me? She almost laughed. —No I'm pretty sure he's moved on.

A few weeks later I began looking for jobs. My resume was weak. I had no real work experience and only two publication credits, two poems and an essay, both in obscure quarterlies. I even fudged it a little—the essay was forthcoming. Nevertheless I applied for every writing and editorial job in the want ads of the major papers. I received no calls in response. Some jobs I applied for week after week, some every day. There was one—editorial assistant at *Guitar World* magazine—I applied for probably a dozen times. No one wanted me. My bankroll dwindled.

My uncle Art's wife—he'd married a much younger woman, close to my age, I could never bring myself to call her my aunt—had a childhood friend who worked in publishing. Her name was Elizabeth and she was an editor at a small children's imprint. Deb put me in touch with her. A lunch was arranged. I met Elizabeth at her office on Astor Place. We walked to a diner called Around the Clock. Elizabeth was tall and blonde, stylish and put-together. She lacked the extra fifteen or so pounds of even the foxiest Michigan babes. As we ate we talked about being new to the city, what the publishing scene was like, what I could do to break in.

—Your mom seems really sweet, she said.

—My mom?

—Yeah. She e-mailed me.

—What?

—Yeah. I assume she got my e-mail from Deb.

—Uh-huh. And what'd she . . . what did she want?

—Oh she just said anything I could do to help you would really be great and if I had any questions or any thoughts I could get in touch with her.

—Questions or thoughts?

—Yeah.

—I see. Well. I guess as long as she's not calling you.

Elizabeth smiled.

—What?

—She called me too.

—Is that . . . did she. And that was what, the same sorta stuff?

—Yeah. Please help my son. I guess she thought I was in a position to hire you or something? I don't know.

I smiled. —Me either.

—You're not mad are you?

—Mad? No. That's not quite the word.

—Good. Because she told me not to tell you. I just figured . . .

She looked at me. —Aw it's not that bad. She's just worried is all. She's looking out for you. It's sweet.

—It's something.

Ninety minutes later I was on the phone with my mother.

—Mom why do you do this?

—What?

—You called that girl, Deb's friend Elizabeth? You sent her e-mails?

—I may have sent her one e-mail. Why?

—*Why?* Are you crazy? Put yourself in my position, then ask yourself why.

—Gee I don't know if I appreciate this hostility—

—You know what I don't appreciate? You always calling around behind my back, meddling in my affairs, trying to arrange things for me.

—I don't always call around—

—How do you think it feels to be talking to someone in New York—a *publishing* person—and suddenly she's telling me my mom's calling her saying—

—Bryan—

—Saying please help my son get a job?

—Bryan I think you need to get a grip here—

—Get a grip? Mom—

—I was just trying to help and you act like it's some terrible thing.

—No. It's not terrible. The Nazis were terrible. This is just . . . I don't even know what this is.

—So now you're comparing me to the Nazis.

—No you're missing the point.

She asked if I'd at least had a good lunch with Elizabeth, if she had any advice or had given me the names any good contacts. I said stop, you're not listening to me, why won't you listen. She said I am listening and asked what was my point. I told her again and again but knew she wouldn't relent and she didn't. We talked in circles a while longer. Then we hung up.

The following week there was a message from Elizabeth asking if I wanted to go to lunch again. I didn't call back. She called one other time. I didn't return that call either. That was the last I heard from her.

One day my dad called. He said he was coming up soon. He was dating a woman in New York. Her name was Marsha. She lived on the Upper West Side.

—It'd be great to see you, he said.

—Yeah.

—I know Marsha'd really like to meet you. I've been telling her about you.

—Is that right?

—Yup-yup. But don't worry. Only the good things.

—Ha. Well that's . . . yeah that sounds good.

—How about next Sunday?

I wanted to say I was busy, make up some excuse.

—Sunday . . . Sunday. No I don't think I have any plans.

I agreed to meet them at Marsha's for brunch. Sunday arrived, bright and windy and cold. I went into the city and found Marsha's building. I stood in the vestibule for a moment, collecting my thoughts. I pressed the buzzer and went in.

I heard my dad before I saw him.

—*Helloooo.*

I climbed the stairs. He greeted me in the hallway. We hugged with hard back slaps. He stepped back, grinning.

—This is Marsha, he said.

She stood in the doorway. She was tallish and thin with incredibly curly shoulder-length black hair. Her apartment was small. There was a table with three chairs and places set. Beyond that was a tiny living room, to the left a tiny kitchen.

—Do you want anything? she asked. —Some coffee or juice?

—I'll have some coffee, I said.

She went into the kitchen. My dad was still grinning, checking me out.

—Look at you. Mr. Big City Guy.

He chuckled, snorted, shook his head. Marsha returned with the coffee. I stirred in some milk. She and my dad stood there grinning. Now they both checked me out.

Marsha asked about my move from Michigan. I rehashed a few new-to-the-city impressions. She smiled along like *oh that's so true.*

—Anyway, she said. —I'll get started on breakfast. Everything's ready, I just have to make the pancakes. You two sit and catch up. I'll be in the kitchen. It should just take a minute.

My dad sat on the little couch. I sat across from him in a chair. Marsha moved around in the kitchen. I heard batter sizzling. My dad and I eased into empty chitchat. We kept it rolling, old pros by now. He chuckled, grinned, shook his head. Marsha reappeared holding a plate of pancakes. She set them on the table and smiled.

—All right, let's eat.

After breakfast we sat in the living room. My dad put his arm around Marsha. They snuggled on the loveseat and talked about how they met—on the Internet, in a chat room for Jewish singles. Marsha said she had their whole relationship documented. She'd saved their e-mails from when they were courting.

—Do you ever go into any chat rooms? she said.

—No.

—No? You've never been?

—No.

—Well. I don't know what your situation is but it's a great way to meet people.

Ten more minutes, I thought, ten more minutes and I'm gone. We exchanged further bullshit. Chitchat lagged. A weird silence fell, broken by Marsha.

—Shoot, she said. —I almost forgot. I have to run to Duane Reade, I'm, I have to get this prescription filled.

She got up quickly, put her coat on, grabbed her purse from the table by the front door. —You guys'll be okay here, right?

—Sure, said my dad.

—Yeah stay and talk. I'm sure you have a lot to talk about so . . . yeah. Who knows how long I'll be, you never know with Duane Reade, they're often, they can be very slow. She smiled. —I'll be back.

Suddenly my dad and I were alone. Big alarm bells rang. I felt a sharp pain in my gut and went into the tiny bathroom. I sat on the toilet but nothing came out. I took deep breaths and splashed water on my face. Back in the living room my dad was still there. He looked at me and smiled.

—What's up? I said.

—No it's just, it's good to see you.

—Good to see you too.

—We oughtta do this more often.

—Yeah.

—But let's not just say it. Let's make it happen this time. Let's really see each other more often.

—All right.

—We really will. We won't let so much time pass.

—All right.

—So what do you think of Marsha?

—What do I think of her? She's . . . yeah. She seems nice.

—Good. Because we're getting married.

We looked at each other.

—Congratulations, I said.

—Thanks, thank you.

He smiled vaguely. His smile faded somewhat.

—Well there's . . . there's something else too.

I knew what it was but waited to hear it.

—We're having a baby.

In the silence that followed I assessed my father. He was fifty-four, maybe fifty-five years old. All our interactions had been like this. They'd never been any other way.

—Wow, I said. —Interesting.

Marsha came in carrying a Duane Reade bag. She hung up her coat, sat on the couch, and smiled. She looked at my dad and then at me.

—So?

I grinned, feigned happiness. You could see relief on their faces. *Everything's fun, this is great, we're pals.* Then the mood shifted. Marsha waxed contemplative. She revealed her age — forty-five — and admitted straight-up this wasn't a planned deal.

Birth defects were a worry. She was moving to DC next month, it was crazy, she never thought she'd leave New York. She knew it was sudden, she knew it must be a shock but I was going to be a big brother and she hoped they'd see more of me, I was part of the family. My dad chimed in. He cosigned the family shit. We sat there gabbing and fake laughing into the mid-afternoon. They said let's grab an early dinner, there's a good Indian place. I tapped unknown reservoirs of strength and said sure. We all got up. Marsha went to the bathroom. My dad came over. He stood close to me and put a hand on my shoulder.

—I know I'm coming at you with a lot here. But I want you to know you're still my son. You're still my number-one guy.

After dinner we stood on the sidewalk. My dad suggested we go for ice cream. I said it was a long ride to Brooklyn and I should probably get back. Marsha said it was great meeting me and gave me a hug.

—We'd love to see you again soon.

My dad stepped up. He flashed the old grin and hugged me with back slaps.

—All right, he said. —Love you.

—Love you too, I said.

I walked two blocks east into Central Park and sat on a bench in the cold. My chest and eyes burned. I rubbed my face. I got up from the bench, walked to Erin's, pressed the buzzer. No answer. I pressed it again. No answer.

I needed to talk to her. She would know how I felt.

Erin's dad left when she was young. Throughout her childhood they were rarely in touch. He had a new family now. He lived in Detroit with his wife and their two middle-school-age sons. Erin loved her brothers but hated her stepmother. She was ambivalent about her dad. The subject could still bring her to fury or tears.

I needed to talk to her. I wanted her to hold me. I wanted to order food with her and watch a movie and not think. I hung around on the stoop and looked up at her window. It was dark. I knew she wasn't home. I lingered another few minutes then walked to the subway.

The train was nearly empty. I sat in the corner and stared into space, feeling at once exhausted and hyper-alert. Tears leaked from my eyes. I couldn't contain them. I put my face in my hands and quietly cried. Why am I so sad? I thought.

The answer was obvious. My dad hadn't wanted me. He never was there for me. Years would pass when he barely called. Now, in his mid-fifties, he's had an awakening. He'll be there for this new kid, he'll stick around. It's not like I wish he'd raised me or anything. No—there's no question I was better off with Ed. Imagine if my dad raised me, what a pussy I'd be. He's a smart guy, sure, knows his Civil War history. But what about the personal history of his own son? Next time maybe. Good luck, old sport. By the way, ever hear of using a condom? Pulling out? Expelling your wad on your Internet girlfriend's stomach instead? As usual the guy's got impeccable timing. Six weeks after I move to New York looking to strike out on my own—certainly the hardest thing I've ever done—along comes my dad again, zapping me back through time, making me feel young and confused and unloved again.

I hated myself for crying over this shit.

Wanted: Marketing Writer

Paul returned to New York in November. He brought another mattress, a thin foam thing from a castoff sofa bed. It was only slightly more comfortable than sleeping on the bare floor. We agreed to switch off—every other night one of us got the good mattress. We placed a single tier of an old brown plastic bookshelf between the two mattresses and loaded it with books and knickknacks. In theory we did this to achieve a modicum of privacy. But it was more a dark comment on our lack of privacy than anything else. Occasionally I'd wake before Paul, look over and stare at him, maybe move around slightly, waiting for him to open his eyes and see me there staring. When he finally did we'd always crack up.

Our last apartment, in Kalamazoo, was on the second floor of a large house. It had a big front porch and expansive views. Even living with Trish—Paul's longtime girlfriend—and a dog and a cat, we had more space than we knew what to do with. One room contained little more than a couch and a phone.

Now we had to brush our teeth in the kitchen sink. We had to walk through Craig's room to get to our room. Neither of the rooms were really rooms.

Craig spent his leisure time lounging on the futon wearing only black boxer briefs. The brand name, printed on the elastic waist, was Winners. He referred to the Winners often and only by this name, as in: the Winners are comfortable, time to wash the Winners etc. Craig stayed up late messing around on the computer. The monitor was the size of the large TV and lit the whole back room, no matter how much he dimmed the brightness. If I was having trouble sleeping Craig's mouse clicks would resonate like hits on a snare drum. The low light of the monitor was like a nuclear blast.

Paul and Craig had moved to the city in the spring, Craig to take a job as a web designer at his college professor's son-in-law's firm. Paul, I'd been told, had vague plans to try acting. Paul hadn't told me this, Trish had. She swore me to secrecy, said he didn't want anyone to know. I wasn't surprised. For all of Paul's bonhomie he was actually quite guarded. His many pals tended to love him hugely without really knowing too much about him. But he and I were close, about as close to each other as we allowed other people to get. We met in 1988 at Blue Lake Fine Arts Camp. Paul went for visual art, I went for creative writing.

I always wanted to be a writer, never anything else. In my banker's box were folders full of poems, short stories, essays, plays. I'd even started writing a screenplay last summer, based partly on my experiences as a substitute teacher. My present goal was modest: publication in a small literary journal. Fame would come later. Maybe not fortune but enough to make a decent living, I was sure of it.

All of this was easier to talk about in Michigan, where I'd had a few compadres who knew the score. My friend Greg and I made a popular local magazine, *Rocket Fuel*. Twice a year we spent hours at Kinko's putting the thing together—copying, collating, stapling. As we went along we'd read our new work aloud, usually poems and funny essays. We continued to make *Rocket Fuel* after Greg moved to Chicago in '95. We made the final issue just before I left for New York.

I understood Paul's reluctance to discuss his ambitions. To reveal even the slightest goal or foggiest plan in a city teeming with actors and writers on all rungs of the ladder seemed at best pretentious, at worst an invitation to bad luck. Here our desires went unexpressed.

And the truth, in a way, was I'd moved to New York not to heed any profound calling but for lack of any better ideas. Most of my friends were leaving Kalamazoo or had already left. When Paul said he was leaving too—that he and Trish were moving out, she was going back to Petoskey to go to nursing school, maybe they'd break up, who could say for sure, he was joining Craig in New York, Craig had found a pad—that was it, the final nail in the coffin. But say the dice had landed differently—say Paul had said hey let's go to Chicago. Most likely I'd be gearing up for another midwestern winter, planning my next move in an apartment in Pilsen or Ukrainian Village.

Paul was flush with dough from his power-plant gig and since technically he'd been laid off he applied for and was granted unemployment. He was in no hurry to find work again and with my job hunt at a dead end we spent many days goofing off in the city. We'd hit the East Village record stores two or three times a week. We'd eat cheap lunches at Dojo on St. Marks Place or at one of the Indian restaurants strung with plastic chili-pepper lights on First Avenue. I'd go to the Strand and leave with at least one half-price paperback each time. I've always needed a lot of books around and mine were all still in boxes in Michigan.

After a few weeks of this my already meager finances were shot. Paul comforted me with tales of his own poverty in the city, which had reached a low point last summer, just before he landed the power-plant job.

—I was living on salads. I tried making pad Thai with a packet of Ramen noodles, crushed peanuts, and soy sauce.

—How was that?

—Horrible. Trish came out in August, I think just to make sure I ate at least a few decent meals.

Paul's grandmother was on government assistance. She sent him a couple big boxes of rations. In our cupboard was a large can with a white label and a silhouette of a chicken. WHOLE CHICKEN, it said. There was also a box of government-issue powdered milk. Paul had eaten the other items before leaving for Jersey.

At the Met Food on Driggs Avenue I loaded my basket with hot dogs and Weaver frozen chicken products—drumstick-shaped nuggets and patties, called rondelets. Nearly all of my meals featured a dipping sauce. Often they came with a side of Herr's barbecue potato chips. I was a gifted maker of beanie-weenies.

I hadn't followed any sort of writing schedule in Michigan. It was more like whenever something came to me I'd sit at the desk. Once I had something down I was content to rewrite endlessly. Revision was my favorite part of the act. Lacking even a desultory work schedule in New York I began to feel useless. So one day when Craig was at work and Paul was out I pulled the large floor speaker Craig used as a chair up to his desk and using his computer wrote for two or three hours. It felt good to be writing. I lost myself in the work. I finished a five-page story about an encounter I'd had many years ago on a hot summer day with a weird girl with scars on her arms who was reading *Naked Lunch* and told me it was her bible. I called the story "Scars," put it through a few rounds of revisions, printed multiple copies, checked my list of addresses, and started sending it out to the little magazines.

* * * *

On the phone my mom asked if I was able to keep body and soul together—one of her favorite expressions.

—Oh yeah. I'm fine.

—Because I can write a check for a few hundred bucks and drop it in the mail first thing tomorrow.

—No no. That's not necessary. I'm good.

—You sure?

—Yeah. I've got a bunch of resumes out. Something's bound to come up.

—All right. Well. Like I say, we're here if you need us.

I'm fine. I'm good. It wasn't true. I was sinking. Faxing resumes daily was a hot ticket to nowhere. December was coming up. Rent and bills would be due. I made an appointment at a temp agency and spent a morning doing their battery of tests. They asked what I was looking for. Anything, I said.

Erin and I rented *Austin Powers* and Chris Rock's *Bring the Pain.* We watched them at her place lounging in bed. Afterward with the lights out we kissed and we took off our clothes. Neither of us had planned on this happening—or that's what we told each other anyway—but now that it had we couldn't seem to stop. Every time we'd pause and say this should really be the last time . . . but there was never a last time and it wasn't like before, it was better, we were a few years older and there was an ease to it now. Still, the implications scared me. How far could we take this? What did she want from me? What did I want from her? I ignored these questions and brushed aside my doubts. I put my hands everywhere and buried my face in her neck. The past was alive in the shape of her body and dead gods spoke to me through her tongue and her mouth.

* * * *

I got a temp job with long-term potential. I worked at a law firm at 120 Broadway entering lawyers' timesheets into a database for twelve bucks an hour. I worked with four women in a tiny office called the Information Center. I sat at a computer and keyed in numbers all day, moving only three fingers of my right hand. On my lunch hour I'd snarf peanut butter and jelly sandwiches from home then wander the tangled grid of streets east of Broadway. If I was feeling rich I'd spring for greasy Chinese food at Win Won, a little place with seating upstairs in an alley off Liberty Street. Most of the time I'd end up at the Strand's Fulton Street Annex or at a place on Nassau Street called SoHo Books that sold overstock and remainders. Sometimes I'd walk to the World Trade Center and read magazines at Borders and walk around the mall. Being in the mall comforted me. It was like being at the Crossroads Mall back in Michigan. It had a lot of the same stores and all the same smells: new clothes, pungent perfumes and lotions, fast food. The weather was weirdly warm that December. A couple times I got a coffee and sat on the plaza watching people and looking up at the towers. There was a holiday display set up between the two buildings, three huge words: PEACE ON EARTH.

Two weeks after I started the other temp quit to pursue acting more seriously. She was replaced the following Monday by a guy named John.

—What'd you do before this? I asked.

—I taught fiction writing.

—Really? Where?

—Arizona State. I was an adjunct. I got my MFA there.

—So you moved here recently?

—A few months ago, yeah.

We started to talk about writing and books. It turned out we dug a lot of the same people. Denis Johnson, Raymond Carver,

Tobias Wolff. I felt a surge of affection for John. At the same time I felt territorial, vaguely jealous, not of his achievements necessarily—aside from his MFA we were roughly equal in that regard—but of his mere presence. There were only so many crumbs at this particular table. If John snagged a few there'd be fewer left for me.

One of the lawyers came in with more timesheets. We divided them up and got back to work.

I'd worked deadening jobs in the past. I worked a summer in the press room at Checker Motors where I stood pressing a button all day, punching out car parts. I worked two summers at the paper mill. I was swing shift there, working sixth hand mostly, which meant being present to help clean and rethread the paper machine when it went down. But when the machine was running well it meant long hours of nothing to do or hours of doing busy work like emptying broke-boxes or wandering the basement spraying down floors and cleaning out rooms that hadn't been entered much less cleaned in years, or simply finding a far-off spot to hole up in and wait for the day or the night to pass. Briefly I worked as a sitter at a hospital, which meant just that—sitting in a room with a sick or injured person if they or their family requested it. I sat in a room with a wide-eyed man in a full body cast and a halo drilled in his skull. He'd been in a car wreck and his mother was there and together we watched a show on cable about the End of Days. The screen showed a series of horrific things but the man and his mother agreed the reality would be far worse than anything we could imagine when the Lord finally came. I sat with a blind amputee who was in a kind of coma, sat horrified and staring at the man's leg stumps and was helpless to stop him when he shoved his hand down his throat and began gagging himself. I'd been told how to stop him if this happened but I was scared and yelled out and the nurses ran in. I watched them work feeling impotent and embarrassed and quit that very night. Long before any of that I washed dishes at the Gull Lake Country Club, the Bayview Gardens, the Gull Lake Cafe. I washed dishes and scrubbed toilets at the Gull Lake View golf course.

The Information Center was worse than all of those things.

My supervisor's name was Gina Vasquez.

—Hey Gina.

—Yeah Bryan, what's up?

—I was wondering what the deal was for Christmas.

—In terms of . . . ?

—Well my friend is driving back to Michigan, where I'm from, and I was thinking it'd be good to go with him, maybe take that week off.

—The week of Christmas?

—Right.

—Hmm. That's a bad week, that's our busy time. We're gonna have a bunch of people rushing to get timesheets in before the end of the year.

—So that's . . . I mean . . .

—You think there's any way you could stick around?

—I don't know. I mean I hadn't planned on it.

—Because, you know, you're doing good here and most likely they're gonna create a permanent data position in the IC. Probably you'd be first on the list. Honestly? You take that week off, I have to get someone else to fill in . . . who knows?

Erin stayed too. We spent Christmas Eve together. I was happy to be with her but succumbed to a malaise. I'd never spent a Christmas away from home. I missed the Michigan winter landscapes, the lake-effect snowstorms, the bitter cold air.

On Christmas morning we had egg sandwiches and coffee from the deli. I bought a Drake's honey bun as a holiday treat for myself. I almost cried talking to my mom and Ed on the phone.

Late in the day we went into the city. We looked at the tree at Rockefeller Center but it was too crowded and we didn't linger. We went to see *The Thin Red Line* at the Ziegfeld. A man behind us was crinkling a peanut bag. Erin asked him politely to stop. The man lunged forward and cursed at her. She left the theater for several minutes and returned still upset.

Meanwhile the movie had affected me strangely. It was a war movie, Terrence Malick's first film in twenty years. The dreamy pace, the voiceovers, the stunning nature shots juxtaposed with battle scenes—it all triggered a stark existential terror.

In this world a man himself is nothing, Sean Penn's character says, and there ain't no world but this one.

I went to the bathroom. My vision receded. I leaned into the sink to keep from fainting. After the movie Erin and I walked down through Times Square. We stopped at a food court for a snack. Two men next to us started screaming at each other. They got in each other's faces and looked ready to take swings. Erin ran out. When I caught up to her she was standing on Broadway with tears in her eyes.

A week later Paul and I were somewhere in Queens. It was my third time in the borough. The first two were related to a job I'd applied for, a staff writing position at the *Western Queens Gazette*. The editor gave me a test assignment covering a community board meeting. The meeting seemed to take decades. I took pages of notes. I wrote the piece that night and faxed it in the next morning. I never heard back.

We walked along on a main road and then arrived at a party. It was a mellow scene. Paul knew some of the people there, I only knew his friend Charles. I spent most of the night wandering back and forth between the living room and the kitchen, phasing in and out of various conversations. I got high on beer and briefly tried making time with a bespectacled girl who wrote porn for a living. But she was more into Paul and I watched with amusement as she made a play for him, knowing he was forever committed to Trish.

Shortly before midnight we gathered around the TV and counted down from ten as the ball dropped in Times Square. Everyone cheered. Paul and I hugged. I'd shed my Christmas malaise and now felt strangely optimistic, not my usual state.

There's something inside me, I know it.

I want my life to be different.

I want to achieve extraordinary things.

Paul and I took a car service home, arriving around one a.m. A short time later Erin arrived. We shot the shit for a while and hit the sack. Erin and I waited till Paul was asleep. Then we slipped into the living room and made out on the futon.

On the Thursday after New Year's Gina came to my desk.

—How would you feel about a little overtime?

—When?

—Tonight. I need you. Just for an hour or two. You see all these timesheets here and they just keep coming in.

I looked at the timesheets and then at the clock. It was almost five.

—You know I can't tonight. I already have plans.

Gina held my gaze for a moment before turning to John.

—What about you?

—Actually I can't stay tonight either.

—Great. Thanks guys.

She shook her head and left the room.

When I got home there was a message from a woman at the temp agency saying my assignment had ended, no need to go in tomorrow. She was still at the office when I called her back.

—What does that mean, my assignment has ended?

—It means your assignment's over.

—Yeah but why? I thought this was supposed to be a long-term thing.

—Apparently what, there was some overtime issue?

—Issue? No. I told her I didn't want to do it.

—Okay. Well. Could that have been the issue?

—I thought it was optional. She said how would you feel about overtime? *How would you feel?* Does that sound dire to you?

—Look all I know is I got a call from Gina saying don't send him back. It happens all the time. It's not a big deal.

—Not a big deal? How am I supposed to live?

—We'll get you something else.

—Okay. Today? Can you get me something today?

—Let me see what I have. I'll give you a call back tomorrow.

The next morning I called the Information Center.

—Gina it's Bryan. Please. Give me another chance.

—Bryan I'm sorry but I need someone in here I can count on. I mean you and that other guy, I had to get rid of him too.

—But I skipped Christmas. I stayed in New York for this job. Silence.

—Gina listen to me. I have three hundred dollars.

She hung up. I stood there seething. Paul came in and suggested we go get breakfast. We walked to the Luncheonette Fountain and ate large platters of eggs and tasteless potatoes for a buck-fifty each.

When we returned the red light on the answering machine was blinking. It was a message for me from the head of the temp agency, a man with whom I'd had no prior dealings. He relayed to me in a borderline shout that I was way out of line calling his clients and I had no right to go telling tales out of school and the agency wouldn't be working with me anymore. I played the message again.

—That is amazing, said Paul.

He brought his four-track recorder into the kitchen. He put a mic up to the answering machine and recorded the man's rant.

Erin's uptown sublet ended. She moved into a loft on Newel Street not far from my pad. Her room was okay but the people she lived with were struggling-musician creeps. The guy next door to her would hole up for hours playing the same idiotic funk bass line over and over again. I'd never known a musician of any kind who could work the same two-second riff so tirelessly. It was maddening.

One night I was lying on her bed contemplating all the things that were going wrong for me. I had no money, no job, no prospects. I'd finished another story and had sent it out but like "Scars" no one wanted it and the rejection slips were coming in.

—I know what'll make you feel better, she said.

—What?

—Put on your shoes, get your coat.

—Where are we going?

—Trust me, she said.

We turned left out of her building and walked to the end of the block. Across the street was a grocery store, a parking lot, and a little cluster of fluorescent-lit shops. Erin led me through the parking lot into a Taco Bell Express. She ordered six regular hardshell tacos and paid for them. We ate them sitting on the floor of her room. She put on a CD to block out the dude's bass. It had been a long time since I'd had Taco Bell and the tacos were good.

—See don't you feel better? she said.

—I really do.

I crunched another taco. She looked at me and laughed.

* * * *

I called my mom but couldn't come out with it right away. Late in the conversation she brought it up, asked how I was doing money-wise. I said I'd lost my temp job and things were bad. She offered to send me a check. I said I didn't want to put them out. She said you won't be putting us out, no we're in good shape, Ed got his big check and he has his pension coming in.

Ed had worked at the paper mill for thirty years. He pushed himself so hard his back eventually gave out. He spent much of the nineties alternating between workers' comp and restricted duty. Management had long been unsure of what to do with him and recently he'd been, in effect, fired. Ed negotiated his own forced-retirement deal. He got to keep his pension and was issued a workers' comp settlement—something like a hundred and fifty grand. I knew this money was the foundation of my parents' retirement and had to last them the rest of their lives. I felt ashamed and guilty asking for any of it. My mom insisted it wasn't a big deal. She express-mailed a check for six hundred bucks. This brought me back up to eight hundred or so. I kept sending out resumes, ten or twelve at a time, barely keeping track of where I sent them anymore.

One Sunday there was an ad in the *Times* classifieds. *Wanted: Marketing Writer* was all it said. I faxed in my resume and cover letter. The next day a man named Tim called and said he wanted to meet with me. Tim's office was on John Street, not far from the law firm. I sat in a folding chair while he studied my resume. His mustache made bristling sounds as he stroked it.

—So Kalamazoo, Michigan, huh? That's really a place?
—Yes it is.
—Funny. I thought it was just that old song.
—No. It's real.
Tim grinned. —Long way from home, huh?

—Yeah I guess so.

—All right so lemme tell you a little bit about my client okay and then we'll talk and we'll see. They're a financial company, they're down here on Wall Street. And they're looking for someone with exactly these . . . qualifications.

The phone rang. Tim answered it, spoke briefly, hung up.

—Sorry about that. So. Like I was saying, my client is a firm, a small mutual fund firm, they're over on Wall Street . . .

He paused and searched my blank face.

—You uh. You know what a mutual fund is, don't you?

—I have to be honest with you, I don't.

Tim sat back. He brushed at his mustache. He studied my resume.

—You know what? That's not a problem at all.

I took the train in early and stood on the corner of Water and Wall Street staring up at a nondescript building. *Black* was about the only thing you could say about it. I was wearing a suit I'd last worn at age fifteen. My mom had overnighted it to me for the sole purpose of this interview. Wall Street, she said, you're gonna wanna look sharp. But the suit was long out of fashion, if it had ever been fashionable in the first place—a big if. The jacket had weird useless buttons on it and now fit tightly everywhere. The sleeves stopped short of my wrists. The pants were too tight and the cuffs rose nearly to my shins when I sat. Over the suit I wore the battered maroon Carhartt I'd been rocking since '93. Frayed threads dangled from the sleeves and waist. On my feet were scuffed black Clarks and white tube socks. I crossed the street and went into the lobby. I took the elevator to the twenty-third floor.

The company was called First Investors. A woman named Clara met me in reception and led me back to her office. She studied my resume. She looked at me and smiled.

—So tell me about yourself.

—Well uh. Let's see. I'm a writer. Um. I just moved here a few months ago—

—That's your main interest, your passion? Writing?

—My passion? Yeah I suppose it is.

She leaned back in her chair.

—I assume you know what we do here.

—Well sure. Yes. I mean I have an idea.

—An idea.

—Yes.

—You know what a mutual fund is?

—I . . . vaguely. But it's like I explained to T—

—And you, let's see.

She looked at my resume.

—You were a substitute teacher in . . . Portage? Teaching . . . sociology?

—Sociology, yes.

—And you have no previous marketing experience, correct?

—That's correct.

I felt my face burning. I was uncomfortable in my suit.

At the end of the interview she thanked me for coming and said they'd be in touch. I walked out of the building feeling shrunken and small.

I'd written the whole thing off by the time I got home but Tim called later and said Clara liked me. They wanted to see me again.

The following week I went back and sat in a large conference room taking an hour-long proofreading test. I turned it in with no hope or despair, figuring now I'd put First Investors out of my mind for good. It had been an interesting diversion but Wall Street wasn't my scene, that was clear. Surely there were other people in the running for the job who actually understood what the job entailed, people with business or marketing degrees. They'd weed me out now, they had to. Good thing I'd been honest with Clara and told her I didn't know shit. I could've gotten in over my head. Things could've gotten out of hand.

Tim called and told me I was really on a roll, I really nailed that test.

—I did?

—Apparently. They want you to come in again.

—They do?

—Yeah. Writing test this time.

—Huh. All right.

—You don't sound too thrilled.

—No I'm thrilled. But . . . another test?

—Yeah but this one's the big one. The writing test. See? You're applying for a job as a financial writer.

—No I know, I get it. It's just, things are getting a little tight here. I don't have a ton of time to play around with, financially speaking.

—Look. Hang in there okay. This looks promising. All you gotta do now is wow em with your writing skills. And that's easy, right?

I laughed. —I guess so.

—Hey. You made it this far.

I went back on a Friday late in the day. I'd been told Clara was out and that I'd be meeting a woman named Samantha. I sat in the waiting area and flipped through a magazine. The receptionist had left and the office seemed still and quiet from out there. She came around the corner. She looked about my age. She had black hair and wore a black suit and was smiling and had a beautiful smile. I stood and shook her outstretched hand. Silently I cursed my suit.

—Hi. I'm Samantha.

She led me down a hall and into a large office. She gestured to a vacant desk in the corner. Next to the computer monitor was a yellow pad, a pen, and a sheet of paper with a single block of text printed on it.

—There's the assignment, she said.

I glanced at the paper and then back at her.

—You can use the computer there. You know how to turn it on?

I looked at it quickly. —Yeah. No problem.

—Anything else you need? Water or anything?

—No I think this should do it.

—Okay. Good luck.

She smiled and turned to leave. She paused and looked at her watch.

—I'm heading out right at five, I have to be somewhere. You can just leave your test on the front desk on your way out.

—The front desk. Got it.

I watched her walk out. The room buzzed with her presence. I could still smell her perfume. I glanced at the test. I was having trouble concentrating. This windowless dead zone had taken on a sexual vibe.

What are you doing here? And where do you have to be?

Two hours later I was sitting on the high barber-style chair next to the so-called counter. Paul was at the stove frying burgers.

—I'm telling you it was jarring. One minute I'm staring at *Financial Planner Weekly* or some shit, the next minute this beautiful girl appears.

—That's how it is in New York. Think of all the beautiful women you see on the street. They all have to work somewhere.

—Yeah but there's something about this place. It just seemed unlikely.

—What was the writing test like?

—I had to write a brochure for a mutual fund.

—Do you know how to do that?

—No. But another applicant's file was out on the desktop. I clicked it open and read it to kinda get some ideas.

The door opened. Craig walked in.

—Burger night, said Paul.

—Sweet. Can I have one?

—Sure.

Craig took his coat off and went to his room. He came back to the kitchen, washed his hands, formed a burger patty, and put it in the pan.

—I'll make some corn. That way it'll be a complete meal.

Craig heated a can of Del Monte corn. He took a head of iceberg lettuce from the crisper, put a few pale leaves in a bowl, and doused them with ranch.

—Anybody else want a salad?

Paul and I declined. We brought our food to the living room and sat with our plates in our laps. We ate our burgers and watched TV.

Erin's birthday party was at a bar on the Lower East Side. Somehow she knew Moby, who came with his pal Damien, a hip painter. Moby bought drinks for the table and took the seat next to me. We exchanged awkward pleasantries. Here was a weird new high-wire act—pretending to be unfazed in the presence of a celebrity while formulating things to say meant to get them to like you, all without revealing your true desperation. I sucked down my drink and tried to relax.

Damien was saying something about a problem with the doorman asking to see some ID and he didn't have any on him.

—I should've just gone to the newsstand and bought a copy of *Vogue* and shown the guy that, that would've fucking proven I was twenty-one.

—Why *Vogue*? I asked.

—Well. There's a big spread on me in the current issue.

More people arrived. I sat with Jonathan, a playwright, and Pete, an actor. I'd met them before and knew them a little but couldn't shake the feeling that I was beneath them somehow. One of Jonathan's plays was in an anthology I'd been assigned in a college playwriting class. Pete had a hilarious scene-stealing cameo in *Living in Oblivion*, a well-known indie flick. The three of us drank and talked about books.

—I'd love to read some of your stuff, said Pete.

—Yeah Charles, said Jonathan, —what the fuck?

I laughed it off. I changed the subject.

At the end of the night we took a cab back to Brooklyn. On the Williamsburg Bridge I turned and looked back. The city lights blinked like a billion earth-stuck stars. In the dark of her bedroom Erin bent down to kiss me. Her hair fell around me and I moved into her and she sighed. I ran my hands over her legs up her waist to her breasts. I love you, I whispered. The words surprised and terrified and thrilled me. I didn't know if I meant them. I didn't know anything. Erin said my name. We moved together in the darkness.

Tim was on the phone again telling me First Investors had narrowed it down to just me and one other guy. He said he'd let me know the minute he heard. I was floored. I never thought for a second I stood a chance at this job. Now that it was a possibility I couldn't think of anything else. I called back the next morning. Still no news. They waited another day and then made their offer: thirty-two thousand a year plus full benefits. I said yes immediately without a word or even a thought of negotiation. I hung up and stood there, high on relief. I called my parents and told them the news. I planned a quick trip home before my start date,

March 8. Somehow I'd done it, I'd saved myself. And had done it in high style. Thirty-two grand was some righteous coin, more than I ever thought I'd make. It's funny the things that change your life. A three-word want ad had delivered me to this precipice. I tumbled headlong over the edge.

The pilot told the flight attendants to prepare for takeoff. This was always the worst moment for me. The engines revved. The plane sped down the runway. My hands were sweating and shaking, my heart was pounding, I struggled for breath. We left the earth and I turned and caught a glimpse of the city. The little towers of the World Trade Center in the distance under a gray winter sky.

Six Feet of Asshole

I sat with my parents at the dinner table in Galesburg, Michigan.

—So you're not gonna end up a derelict after all, said Ed.

I laughed. —You never know. I still might.

—No, said my mom. —You did it. You pulled a rabbit out of your hat.

—With some help from you guys.

—We were happy to do it. Weren't we, honey?

—Yes dear, said Ed in his fake-compliant voice.

—See. I have him trained.

—Impressive.

—What are you gonna be doin at this place? said Ed.

—Writing and editing marketing materials.

—What the hell's that mean?

—Brochures, letters, things like that. Basically whatever needs to be written.

—A-ha. Sittin on your ass in other words.

—No it's hard work, said my mom.

—Hard work. Shit. I'll show you hard work. Follow me around the mill for a couple days.

—Honey we can't. You're retired.

—I know about the mill, I said. —I worked there too.

—Yeah. For a summer.

—Two summers.

—Boy I'm not knockin it. I'm serious. I woulda loved to've sat around on my ass and taken home a big paycheck.

—You're gonna need some clothes, said my mom.

—I know. I don't think my old suit's gonna cut it.

—Ed has some clothes you can have, some old shirts and ties.

—Well now wait a minute.

—What? Honey you don't wear that old stuff. You haven't worn it in years.

—Yeah but the point is it's mine. It's there if I need it.

My mom looked at me. —He's kidding.

—I know.

Ed nudged me. —See. She has me trained.

I drove around Gull Lake. It was all gray ice. I drove through Richland and turned right at the light, past the Parkview Cafe and the Village Drug. The road curved to the left and went by the old intermediate school, long empty. I drove down M-43 to Gull Road, past Meijer's Thrifty Acres, the East-Towne Mall, Frosty Boy, New Horizon Village. I entered Kalamazoo where virtually every house and street corner called out to me speaking of some old dream or trouble or triumph or heartache. My mom had left my old tapes in the car. I'd put one in and was singing along. *Whenever whenever whenever I feel fine I'm gonna walk away from all this or that.* The trees were skeletal, the skies were swollen, the color of steel. The roads and parking lots salted white.

I walked into the Water Street Coffee Joint. Bits and Zoe were there.

Bits and I were the last of our circle to leave Kalamazoo. Last summer we'd spent many evenings together, drinking coffee at Blake's Diner and taking aimless amped-up walks around town. Bits split for Minneapolis around the time I moved to New York.

He'd gotten a job as an art teacher and was now painting and playing in a new band. Zoe was still in town, finishing her last year at Western.

—How's Craig doing? said Bits. —Still pulling out his dick all the time?

I laughed. —Not as much these days. But yeah. Sometimes.

—Yeah that guy can't resist. What about Paul?

I told him about Paul's power-plant gig and all the bread he saved.

—What's he gonna do when it runs out?

—I don't know. Get another job I guess. He's still on unemployment so it's not an issue yet. He and Trish were having problems. They broke up for a little while.

—Shit, really?

—Yeah. They've been working it out. She's talking about moving to New York.

Bits laughed. —All of Kalamazoo's gonna be out there soon.

They sat holding hands. They said they'd been talking about marriage. Zoe was moving to Minneapolis when she was done with school—maybe they'd get married a year or two after that.

—Marriage, I said. The word sounded crazy to me.

—Hey, said Bits. —When you know you know. We've been together five years. What are we gonna do, wait around? Start dating again? No.

—Has it really been five years?

—Yeah.

—What about you, Skip? said Zoe. —Do you have a lady?

—No. I don't know.

—What about Erin? said Bits. —You ever see her?

—Yeah. I see her.

My mom went through Ed's closet pulling out his old dress clothes. There weren't many and they were all from the seventies or early eighties. I got a light blue shirt, a brown tie, and a pair of gray dress pants. This brought my work wardrobe up to two shirts and two ties. The pants were far too big in the waist but I took them because they were my only business-dress option. I only owned two pairs of pants—a pair of jeans and a pair of khakis. I'd bought the khakis for fifteen bucks at Old Navy and wore them every day at my law-firm job. At First Investors I'd wear them on Casual Friday. The castoff grays would get me through the other four days, rotating my limited shirt-tie combinations, until I saved up some money for new threads.

I flew back to New York on a Sunday. My mom and Ed stood watching me pass through security. It reminded me of the day I'd left town five months ago, standing by the train tracks waiting for the train to pull in. You make a good life for yourself there, Ed had said when he hugged me. I'd cried as the train left Kalamazoo. I had the same sad feeling now: I'm leaving something good here, leaving my family behind. I sat waiting for my flight, a little puddle jumper to Detroit, thinking, please get me through this, please let me live. As the plane took off I stared out at the snow-bright landscape, wishing I was staying in Michigan where at least I knew who I was.

My first assignment at First Investors was a piece for an investor education series called *Thinking Primarily About . . .*

Because I'd made no secret of my ignorance of the industry Clara thought it'd be good for me to dive right in and learn as I went along. Trial by fire, she said. I was to write "Thinking Primarily About Mutual Funds."

—Start by seeing what else is out there. We have a file of competitors' materials. Boom. Right there. First stop. Read those materials, get a feel for the language. Learn how other people write about mutual funds, how they explain them to novice investors. In a way it's great, right, because you're your own audience. You don't understand mutual funds so you'll be able to write about them in a way the average reader can understand. Talk to Peter. He can help. Talk to Samantha.

I wrote down everything she said on a First Investors notepad. I left her office and returned to my desk. I didn't know how or where to begin. I looked at my notes and saw only the word *Samantha*.

Blue-gray cubicle walls about shoulder-high. Light-blue plastic desktop. Khaki-colored monitor and keyboard with black grime in the keys. Gray metal desk drawers. Blue-gray adjustable uncomfortable office chair. Two items from home: a James Dean calendar my mom sent me for Christmas and a Chock full o'Nuts can in which I stored pens. The desk was too low and forced me to hunch. I stuck a phone book under the monitor and that helped a little. Seven hours of sitting. I remembered the feeling of it from the law firm but now I was also closed in. Seven hours of sitting.

Are you ready? Begin.

A new print of *Days of Heaven* came to the Film Forum. Erin and I went with Remington opening weekend. We were first in the ticket-holders' line, which soon stretched down the block. It was a cold night. We waited outside for twenty minutes or so. A little before showtime an usher opened the door preparing to let people in. As he did so two women rose from a bench in the lobby. They walked outside and stood in front of us. We looked at each other and then at these women, who stared ahead blankly as if nothing unusual had occurred. I tapped the one closest to me on the shoulder.

—Excuse me but are you cutting?

—Cutting? No. We have our tickets. We wait in there.

She gestured inside. She was olive-skinned and stylish, as was her friend. She had a European accent of some kind.

—No I know. I saw where you were waiting. But you see we were here in this line before you.

—Please, said the woman as she turned away from me.

Erin and Remington grinned. I tapped her again.

—We, all of us here, we've been standing in the cold. You were in there in the warm lobby. Do you think that's fair?

—Fair? What do you mean? Why don't you give me a break.

—No. No I'm sorry. But I have to insist that you move to the end of the line.

—I am not moving. Okay. I was here.

—No you weren't. I pointed at the bench in the lobby. —You were in there.

The usher had been watching. He stepped out and listened.

—He's right. I saw you guys inside. You're gonna have to move to the back of the line.

—Jesus Christ, said the woman.

She and her friend stepped out of line. The woman turned and got in my face.

—You! she said loudly. —You are an asshole. However tall you are, that is how much asshole you are. You are six feet of asshole!

The line grew quiet. Everyone stared. The blood roared in my head.

—Six-five, I said.

I received a box of business cards that said BRYAN A. CHARLES, STAFF WRITER. I sent one to my mother and she was delighted. I started reading the *Wall Street Journal* and various financial websites, learning the biz. I made sure Clara saw the *Journal* open on my desk every morning. Occasionally if I felt comfortable I'd mention an article or some topic of interest to the markets generally.

I ran drafts of my "Thinking Primarily About Mutual Funds" piece by Peter, the senior writer. He was in his early thirties, had been at the game a while, and had a great gift. Peter could open his mouth and speak fully formed marketing sentences. But there was an irony in his manner that subtly conveyed the absurdity of our task. Peter taught me that financial services involved pushing and repackaging and reselling the same few concepts: diversification, buying a new home, saving for your children's college education or your own retirement. But the bedrock tenets of financial marketing were stressing the importance of taking a long-term view and encouraging investors to consult financial advisors.

Part of me dug this wild new scene. I liked getting up early, putting on a shirt and tie, taking a crowded 4/5 downtown. I liked walking down Wall Street in the cool city mornings in the rush-hour crowd, past the Stock Exchange and Federal Hall. I liked stopping for coffee at Biankee's deli and sipping it at my desk in the still-quiet office as I flipped through the *Journal*. I liked roaming the streets on my lunch hour staring at the frenzied men and women in suits, knowing I'd pass for one of them if they glanced my way, which they never did.

Part of me dug this. But another part—barely a ripple then—feared this job was a trap that would overtake me completely.

I began to sweat heavily. It would start on the subway in the morning, a little underarm pinprick, a trickle. By the time I reached my desk sweat would be dripping down my sides and would have soaked through my T-shirt. I'd go into a stall in the men's room and wipe my armpits with paper towels. This solved the problem for three or four minutes. Finally I started folding paper towels and leaving them bunched under my arms at all times. But even that didn't stem the flow. I'd sit at my desk with my arms out and locked in strange uncomfortable positions to avoid staining my dress shirts. This would cause the damp towels to fall out and get lodged at my waist.

I went to Century 21 and bought several packs of new T-shirts. Every day I brought one or two to work with me in a laptop carrying case. I'd stop at various restrooms on my lunchtime walks—the Ranch 1 on Water Street was my favorite. I'd change into a new T-shirt and stuff the soiled one in my bag. Depending on the day I might need to change again in the afternoon. I used the restroom of the Au Bon Pain in the building lobby for this purpose. Before long all my T-shirts had huge yellow-brown stains under the arms and coffee-colored drip marks on the sides.

I researched the issue.

Excessive sweating was known medically as hyperhidrosis. Several heavy-duty antiperspirants were available, including one so badass it required a prescription. These were applied at night and worked by shrinking the pores under your arms as you slept. Another option was surgery. They could burn off a nerve in your spinal column somewhere, thereby shutting down the brain signal that triggered underarm sweat. The problem was a side effect called compensatory sweating, which meant you'd just start sweating more elsewhere—your ass, for instance.

I debated which was worse—wet pits or wet ass.

I would never have had elective nerve surgery but bone-dry pits and wet ass sounded like an absolute dream.

In the Monday morning status meetings I took useless notes and stared secretly at Samantha. She sat two cubicles down from me. We'd talked a few times. She was dating a rich creep who sent her roses at work with little cards that said things like You're beautiful. He was funding a start-up at the moment, a magazine devoted to celebrity pets.

—Celebrity pets? I said. —Interesting.

She laughed. —Is it? The first cover is Renee Zellweger's dog.

—I'll be on the lookout for that.

—I'm sure you will. Can I ask you something?

—Yeah.

—What do you do every day at lunch?

—What do I do?

—Yeah. You leave with that bag. What's in there, a computer? What do you do, go somewhere and write?

—I just . . . I go and take care of things.

—Yeah? What things? Are you writing a novel?

—Maybe.

I walked to my desk and sat for a minute. Then I stood and went to the men's room. I walked behind the cubicles so Samantha wouldn't see me. I wiped out my armpits and put some new paper towels up there. I sat on the toilet collecting my thoughts.

Weeks passed. Erin and I continued to talk on the phone and see each other almost daily. Sometimes we made out, more often we didn't. We rarely discussed what was or wasn't going on with us romantically and whenever we did the conversation was protracted and inconclusive. I sensed she was seeing other guys or at least going on scattered dates and it made me jealous. At the same time I had Samantha on the brain nonstop. We'd upped the ante on our workplace flirting but she was still seeing the rich boy and I had no hope of breaking through.

I was still trying to write but most days couldn't get anything done. Most days it was all I could do to read a few pages in bed before passing out. I'd racked up quite a few rejections slips for the file. Some were encouraging, more than mere form notes. I got nice handwritten comments from *Glimmer Train* and *Story*. I immediately sent them new work. It was returned in both cases with form notes, without even a scrawled set of initials in the corner. I'd been told actual handwriting on a rejection slip was a good sign so I savored—clung to—those few handwritten lines. I'm getting closer, I thought, it's happening.

One morning I walked into the lobby behind Clara. She held the elevator for me. I stepped in and said thanks. We were the only ones in there. She said good morning and I said it back and then there was silence. I looked up at the numbers and then at Clara. I followed her gaze down to my feet and my sad-looking Clarks. The leather was worn and the laces were frayed. My big toe had broken through the right shoe and a speck of white tube sock peeked out. Clara said nothing but the look on her face told me I couldn't put off buying new threads any longer.

I went to Shoe Mania and bought some new Clarks. I went to Today's Man on Sixth Avenue and charged two ties, two shirts, two pairs of pants, five pairs of black dress socks, and a navy blue suit. The suit itself cost three hundred bucks. The total expense was the most I've ever spent on clothes. Still, I knew Today's Man was for geeks and not stylish and I took pains to make sure my ties never flipped over or my suit jacket never fell open in such a way that any labels were visible.

I met Erin after work. We took the train out to Queens, to Jonathan's crib. Pete was there, the actor, as was a pretty, pixieish girl I didn't know. Her name was Stuart. She was an actor too. I gathered from their talk that she had a part in the new Stanley Kubrick film, the last one he finished before his death. Hearing this made me too nervous to speak to her but it didn't matter anyway because Stuart didn't look at me or address me. I sat listening to everyone talk in my cheap work clothes feeling like the ultimate fucking square. Three months earlier I would've felt out of my depth here but now that I worked at an investment company in a cubicle? Forget it.

* * * *

Friday afternoon I stood rapping with Samantha. She glanced at the time in the corner of her monitor.

—Shoot. Almost five.

—Why shoot?

—I have a lot of stuff to do. I'm going to the MoMA after work to buy a gift certificate for my brother. What about you, any weekend plans?

—Me? Nah.

—Nothing? she said.

—Going straight home tonight to rest up for Monday.

—You wanna come with me?

—To the MoMA?

—Yeah. It'll just take a sec.

—What, you have plans afterward or something?

—I do. I'm meeting Nate.

—Nate. Now why would I go all the way uptown with you just to watch you run a two-second errand and then run and meet Nate?

—I'm not meeting him till later. We might have time for one drink.

We went to a restaurant on Fifty-fourth Street called the Typhoon Brewery. We sat at the bar and ordered pints. I drained mine immediately. The bartender came and I ordered another. Samantha drank hers slowly but ordered a second as well. Talk flowed easily. We swapped biographies.

She spent her early childhood in Colorado but really grew up in New Jersey, where they'd moved for her dad's job. He was in waste management. This wasn't a euphemism for the mafia—he actually worked at a company that developed industrial garbage-treatment and recycling systems. She told me Entenmann's products were made in part from old Entenmann's products. They gathered unsold items from grocery store shelves and pulverized and reincorporated them into new batches of baked goods.

—Jesus. Is that even legal?

—Ask my dad.

—I love their Ultimate Crumb Cake.

—Disgusting, she said.

She had an older brother named Jake and younger sister named Eve. She'd gone to college for a year in Vermont and then transferred to Lehigh, in Pennsylvania. She was twenty-five, almost twenty-six. She'd been at First Investors for a year already and she hated it. They were too small, they paid shit, she didn't feel challenged there. She knew she could do a more interesting job for more money somewhere else.

And what about Nate?

Well he was nice, he treated her good, maybe a little too good actually, he doted, was a clinger. Maybe even a little weird-looking. He had a strange mouth. Like this: she lifted her nose with a finger and her front teeth appeared in the gap that opened between her lips. I laughed.

—What about Erin? she asked.

—Erin and I, it's complicated.

—How so?

—We've known each other a long time.

—You dated in Michigan?

—We did, for a year. I was twenty-one.

—A year's a long time.

—For a while I thought she was the one for me forever.

—What happened?

—Nothing really. The fire went out. And then it was more like we were just good friends. And then we broke up. A while after that she moved to New York.

I didn't tell her we'd restarted the fire or that few people knew me the way Erin did. I didn't tell her there were still days when I thought Erin was the one.

—Did you move here because of her?

—Not because of her, no. But she was . . . without her I might not've made it. I might not be sitting here.

—Where might you be?

—I don't know. Back in Michigan living in my parents' basement or something.

—Should we get another round?

—That depends. What time are you meeting Nate?

She looked around for a clock. —We still have some time.

My hand slipped into hers. I touched her leg. Samantha looked down.

—It'd be weird if we kissed, she said.

—What? I said, though I'd heard her perfectly.

She said it again.

I leaned in and kissed her.

We sat kissing at a small table next to the payphone. Occasionally someone walked by going in or out of the restroom. Finally Samantha stood and called Nate. I listened to her tell him that something had come up, she wouldn't be able to meet him. She apologized several times and hung up.

—I think he's mad at me, she said.

—Gee that's a shame.

We went back to the bar for a final drink.

It was a warm bright night. Little white Christmas lights were strung in some trees in a recessed plaza on Fifty-fourth Street. We stood on the corner of Madison and Fifty-fourth and we kissed. She had to be up early tomorrow. She was going to Saratoga Springs for her sister's college graduation. She hailed a cab, kissed me one last time, and got in.

I watched the cab disappear. I lingered on the corner grooving on the people, the buildings, the lights. I took the 6 to Union Square. I walked along Fourteenth Street and turned off on Avenue A. Paul was standing in the crowd outside Brownie's.

—Where have you been?

—Making out with Samantha.

—Nice. Erin's inside. She's been looking for you.

We lay on a sheet on Central Park's Great Lawn. The air was filled with voices and laughter and kid sounds. On the diamond behind us shirtless men played softball. Samantha lay on her back with her eyes closed, her face to the sun. I was perpendicular to her, lying half off the sheet, my legs and bare feet in the grass. It was a Saturday, a week after our first kiss. We'd been here a half hour or so. We'd been talking and laughing but now we were quiet. I put my hand on her stomach and rested it there a moment. I pulled up her shirt, not much just an inch or two. The skin there was golden and shiny with little beads of sweat. Sweat had pooled in her belly button. I watched her stomach rise and fall with each breath. I streaked some sweat drops with a finger and lay my palm on her stomach. I moved it down slowly till my index finger slipped a fraction of an inch under the waist of her shorts, moved it back up till I met the rise of her ribs. I leaned up and kissed her stomach. She inhaled sharply. I let my lips linger there tasting her sweat. She exhaled slowly and placed a hand on her forehead. We gathered our things and walked out of the park. In her room with the door closed we lay on her bed and kissed. The air conditioner hummed and cooled the small space. The early evening light turned everything electric blue.

* * * *

I was on the phone with Erin. She asked how work was going.

—Good. Boring I guess but generally all right.

—Aren't you going to some thing soon, a conference?

—Convention.

—Convention. Where? Puerto Rico?

—Yeah. I'm leaving . . . shit, I leave Friday.

—Puerto Rico, huh? What goes on down there?

—It's gonna be a lot of work actually. A lot of meetings.

—Everyone from your department goes?

—Most people, yeah. The company pays for everything. They put us up in this fancy hotel. I think we get maybe an hour off a day, two, I don't know.

—When are you coming back?

—The fourteenth. I'll send you a postcard.

—A postcard?

—No I'll call you. I'll be in touch.

Samantha and I sat with Jeff, the First Investors' graphic designer, at an outdoor tequila bar on the roof of the El San Juan Hotel. Below was the beach and the crashing surf, the ocean loud and invisible in the night. We were the first of the marketing people to arrive. Everyone else was due in tomorrow.

For the last month I'd worked ceaselessly on convention litera-ture: meeting and dinner agendas, travel-guide-worthy descriptions of local attractions, bio blurbs for the top-performing reps, for whom the convention was a reward. Some nights I worked late and a black Lincoln towncar would ferry me home.

We settled the tab after one drink each. We took the elevator down and said goodnight. I went to my room and killed a few minutes. Then I picked up the phone and dialed Samantha. We spoke for a moment, laughed, hung up.

Then I left and walked to her room.

* * * *

I was wrong about having only an hour or two off a day. It was the opposite—we only worked an hour or two a day. Typically that meant sitting at a desk in the hotel lobby signing the reps up for various activities or stuffing packets or organizing awards plaques in a windowless conference room in the basement. The rest of our time was spent lounging on the beach or by the swimming pool, drinking free cocktails and eating free meals, usually steak or lobster, and in Samantha's and my case, fucking. We fucked every spare moment in those sweet cool rooms on those king-size beds. One evening we fucked on her balcony with a First Investors party in full swing below. A poolside Caribbean Carnival Festival. Business-casual dress. An awful cover band playing eighties radio hits. We were supposed to be there. Instead we were up in a deck chair. Samantha was on top of me. I gripped her ass and looked past her out at the ocean and the sky. *All alone I have cried silent tears full of pride.*

In a downstairs game room we played Ms. Pac-Man. Samantha beat me several times in a row. We switched to air hockey. She won the first game and the next one and the next one. Something came over me and I hit the puck so hard it shot off the table, flipped through the air, and fell clattering to the floor.

—Whoa, she said.

I walked out of the game room. She followed me up to my room. I lay on the bed and stared out the window. I wiped at the tears that streaked my face. Samantha sat next to me. I lay there crying. She looked at me till I met her gaze.

—What's the matter?

I told her about my father. He left when I was very young. I have no real kid memories of him. My clearest memories of him begin when I'm ten, when I flew out to visit him in Washington DC. My mom met Ed when I was six. He moved in with us quickly and two years later we left Kalamazoo and moved out to Galesburg. They got married in an office at the Kalamazoo County Building on a freezing night in December of '87. Somewhere around my early teen years my dad took a greater interest in me. He started calling more, wanting to talk, wanting me to come visit. He'd met a woman named Catherine. She was a doctor. She was Jewish. He converted to Judaism. They got engaged. He asked me to be the best man at the wedding. I didn't want to do it but said yes anyway. My mom took me downtown and bought me my first suit. I was fifteen years old. Two years later he flew to Michigan for my high school graduation. He stood next to me grinning and we posed for pictures. After the ceremony he met my girlfriend Daisy and some of my friends. It felt strange to have him there and to smile with him in those pictures. I'd long ago come to think of Ed as my real dad. At some point Catherine got cancer. They operated but it came back. A few years later she died. I learned she was dead a week after the fact. Almost a year after that my dad called and said a memorial service was being held and asked if I wanted to come out for it. I didn't know Catherine well and hadn't liked her much anyway but my mom encouraged me to go. She said my dad had always been a lonely closed-off person and now that Catherine was dead and his mother was dead I was all he had left. In DC I learned we weren't actually invited to the memorial service. Details were murky. It seemed my dad and Catherine had split sometime before she died. She'd traveled a lot those last couple years and spent most of her time with her sister's family in South Carolina. At the service we sat at a table in back with one of her colleagues from work. There were spiral-bound remembrance packets with a color-copied photo of Catherine smiling on the front. After I was back in Michigan my dad called and said there was something he had to tell me. He was depressed, he'd always been depressed and that was partly why he'd been such a bad father. But he'd turned a corner and was getting better now.

He was in therapy now, taking antidepressants. I didn't know what to say so I just listened and after a while we hung up. Later that year I moved to New York and was trying to figure things out when he called and asked me to come to breakfast and meet his new girlfriend who'd heard so much about me. Two hours after meeting this woman I learned they were getting married and I was going to have a brother and that they hoped I'd be up for being a part of their family. The baby was born in the spring. My dad had e-mailed me photos.

—You should call him, said Samantha.

—Who?

—Your dad.

—I don't think so.

—Why not?

—I don't know. I just don't want to.

—Don't you wanna have a relationship with him someday?

—Maybe someday. Not right now. I'm tired of dealing with his bullshit. I'm tired of it being awkward and strained every time we see each other. I'm tired of him always saying he wants to have some big talk with me and it's always just bullshit because the talk never comes.

—Yeah but now you have a little brother.

—Half brother.

—Bryan.

—Yes.

—He's your brother. What's his name?

—Avi.

—Wow. Your dad really went all out on the Jewish thing.

I laughed. —Oh yeah. He's serious, goes to temple, the whole bit.

—I'm not even that Jewish. And I'm Jewish.

—Maybe I should convert.

—You should. You and Avi could go to Hebrew school together.

    —Avi, I said.

    —Don't you wanna meet him?

    —No.

The rich boy was still after her. He sent her room-service break-
fasts and called three or four times a day. She played me his
anxious voicemails as we lay in bed together and we had a good
old chuckle. Finally she buzzed the front desk and told them to
block his calls. I bought some postcards in the lobby. I sent one
to my mom, who was born in Puerto Rico. I meant to send one
to Erin. I never did.

Samantha and I rotated back to New York hot and heavy. Erin
and I had stopped making out but I didn't have the guts to tell her
about Samantha and just being around her now filled me with
guilt. But I had a little breathing room because Samantha had a
share house down the Jersey Shore and was gone most weekends.
She gave me a key to her pad and I stayed there a time or two to
get away from the cramped scene at my place. One day I was
watching TV there and saw Stephen, Erin's ex, on VH1. I mentioned it to Erin the next time we talked.

    —Where'd you see that? she asked.

    —Where? VH1.

    —Yeah but where? You don't have cable.

    —Oh. Just . . . over at a friend's.

    —What friend?

    —The girl I work with. Samantha.

    —When were you hanging out with her?

    —Well you know I wasn't really, I was—she was out of town
for the weekend and she let me stay at her place.

    —You stayed at her apartment?

—She was out of town. It was hot. She has air conditioning.

—Bryan what's going on with you and this girl?

So began a weeklong series of conversations in person and over the phone, culminating in a ninety-minute blowout on the Fourth of July. It had been a hot, humid day. Night brought no relief. Paul and Craig were out at a party somewhere. Samantha was in New Jersey. I stood in the kitchen sweating and talking to Erin on the apartment's one phone, wishing the conversation was over and I was lying down in the back room where the other day we'd installed the window AC unit we'd all chipped in for.

Erin was crying. She told me it was shitty how I led her on and had sex with her but didn't ever want to commit and then got all possessive and moody and jealous when she hung out with other guys. I didn't argue or disagree. I stood mutely in the kitchen as she yelled and cursed and fireworks boomed, filling the haze over the city with dull flashes of color. Finally she seemed to exhaust herself. I was already exhausted and the moment arrived when there was nothing left to do but hang up.

—I love you, she said in a small strangled voice.

I waited a moment and said it back.

Knock Knock

The summer passed. It was very hot. I stayed with Samantha almost every night. Invariably one of three songs — "Every Morning" by Sugar Ray, "Livin' la Vida Loca" by Ricky Martin or "All Star" by Smash Mouth — would wake us when the clock radio clicked on. We'd take the train downtown, walk down Wall Street together, take turns going first into the office. We'd sleep in on weekends, go to brunch, read the Sunday *Times,* lie on a sheet in Central Park, maybe go to a movie. Sometimes I'd wake early and run out for egg sandwiches, coffee, the paper. The Upper East Side on weekend mornings was quiet and had a strangely small-town feel.

I went with Samantha down the shore a few times. Her roommates in the house were mostly strangers, twenty- and thirty-something professionals who talked up four-beer Saturday-night highs as if they'd stayed up shooting speedballs. Samantha and I sat apart from them on the beach. I'd look over at her dozing in her black bikini and think of the things I'd been doing a year ago — playing in a band with Bits, writing freelance A&E stories for the *Kalamazoo Gazette,* living alone in an apartment with no furniture after Paul and Trish split. It all seemed like it had happened to somebody else.

Samantha and I were together twenty-four hours a day. In the beginning, at work, there was a nominal level of remove, two cubicles separating us. Then someone was promoted and a reshuffling occurred. They moved Samantha to the cubicle next to mine. I didn't mind. I found it helped to pass the time, especially the interminable soul-killing afternoons. We were even assigned a lengthy task together once — proofreading the new prospectuses. One of us was to read aloud while the other followed along. We went into the little conference room, locked the door, and made out, stopping whenever we heard movement in the hallway.

"Thinking Primarily About Mutual Funds" went through round after round of edits. Yet when the final version was printed months later it didn't differ significantly from the third draft. My next piece, "Thinking Primarily About Bonds," was taking even longer to wind its way through the approval process. When I mentioned this to Peter he told me a piece he'd written about elderly investing had been stuck in turnaround since he'd started the job a year and a half ago and was currently in its fifteenth draft. Week after week we went to the status meetings and discussed the status of the same stalled projects. We ticked through the spreadsheet, listening and nodding as if there were new information. Clara then issued the same directives, as if she'd never uttered these words to us before, and we returned to our desks and sat trying to look busy for another week.

Craig moved out in August. Paul and I split the cost of materials and he built a wall with a door between the two back rooms. Things were strained between us. A cloud hung over the pad. His money had run out and he was just scraping by but he made no move to get a job or do much of anything really. I began to resent him sitting around or sleeping in while I was either fried from a workday or getting up to go do it again. Paul caught the vibe and gave me wide berth. We rarely had issues with each other and never discussed them when we did. Passive-aggressive weirdness was more our scene.

Meanwhile he and Trish were back on. A couple times she called while he was out and we talked. She missed Paul bad. She was living alone in Petoskey, working as a waitress at La Señorita, taking nursing classes at community college. She was worried about Paul. She thought he was drifting. She thought she could help get him back on track if she was out here too. At the same time she urged me to be more patient and large-hearted with him. She reminded me that Paul was my best friend and that he always had my back. She reminded me of the summer of '97, just after I graduated college, when I was unemployed and sat around reading six hours a day. I had enough bread saved to cover the rent but that was about it. Paul and Trish floated me. They took me to movies, bought me meals and drinks at the bar, and never judged me or vibed me out when they came home from work and saw me on the couch reading or playing guitar.

Trish was right. I was being too hard on Paul, taking myself and my Wall Street career too seriously. I lightened up. We took a road trip together, drove the van to Michigan over Labor Day weekend. Paul dropped me off in Galesburg and headed up to Petoskey. He returned a few days later and helped me load the rest of my things. We drove through the night, stopping only in a downpour to sleep for an hour in a gas station parking lot in nowhere Pennsylvania. Finally I had a desk and my computer in the city. Now that Paul and I had separate rooms I had my own space to write.

Since starting my job I'd written fifteen pages. Seven of these were a story beginning that went nowhere that I'd cranked out one weekend on Samantha's roommate's computer when they were both out of town. The other eight were aimless one- or two-page bits written whenever I had a free afternoon. Between a girlfriend and a full-time job I found I didn't have the time or energy required to produce a short story or even a decent draft of one. I unearthed the pages of the screenplay I'd started but found that even straight dialogue was beyond me. I needed something I could produce in a blast of language in a single sitting. I stopped reading fiction and read and wrote poetry exclusively. I set a schedule: three nights during the week and a Saturday or Sunday afternoon. My goal at each sitting was to finish a draft of a poem. I worked like a dog, kept to the schedule, and the pages piled up. I picked the most promising poems and revised them while continuing to write more. Weaker poems I either scrapped entirely or cannibalized for a line or two for use in other poems. I sent the poems to the little magazines and tracked my submissions in a spiral notebook. If I missed a writing day I was at best slightly anxious and at worst horribly depressed. Samantha spent a lot of time talking me through these fits. If I kept to the schedule and met my daily goal I was generally all right.

But there were other times, the bad times, when I sat at the desk and the words wouldn't come and I'd curse my fate and wonder why it had to be like this, eight, nine at night and me just now sitting down to write, already exhausted, knowing my mind was clearest and I wrote best in the morning. I'd stare at the blinking cursor with burning eyes and everything would hit me at once—the fatigue, the rejection, the hours wasted in my cubicle going over the bonds piece again, putting in commas at one person's request, taking the same commas out at the request of someone else.

In brighter moments I was able to convince myself that my First Investors writing in some way improved my real writing, helped me sharpen and make clearer what I wanted to say, stripping away all excess like Hemingway or Joan Didion. I'd think of Don DeLillo, who worked in the ad game when he was starting out, doing more or less the same shit. It was a tenuous delusion and collapsed like a house of cards at the slightest puff of air.

—I wanna do something I believe in to make money. Something I love, you know?

—Yeah but th—

—I don't wanna sell fucking tacos.

—Paul you're not—

—I mean is that just me? Am I being unrealistic?

—I don't know. Maybe.

—I thought about trying to rent a little studio or something somewhere so I could get back to painting or drawing again. But everything was too expensive and that just bummed me out more.

We drove along on the BQE. At Meeker Paul exited and looked for a parking spot. We crossed Nassau and entered an industrial strip just west of our block. Shuttered warehouses, large empty truck lots, no people. Ahead of us the Citibank tower in Long Island City rose out of nothing, looking grotesquely out of place.

—You're not gonna have to sell tacos, I said.

I kept grinding out poems. They kept coming back rejected. I dug up more addresses, little lit mags I'd never heard of at small colleges in the middle of nowhere. Greg—my old *Rocket Fuel* collaborator who now lived in Chicago—sent me an e-mail with a link to a website called *McSweeney's*. They published short humor pieces, including a couple of Greg's. I read through the site. Experimental whimsy tinged with bland sarcasm seemed to be their MO. They published a physical magazine too. I went to St. Mark's Bookshop and bought the current issue. My stories didn't seem quite right for them but I dusted one off, gave it a mild rewrite, and sent it in anyway. I never heard back.

* * * *

I spent Thanksgiving at Samantha's parents' house in Roseland, New Jersey. Her dad built a fire and all the lighting was just right. The rooms were cozy and tastefully decorated. We sipped wine and munched hors d'oeuvres as the food cooked. The house slowly filled with wonderful smells.

Her brother Jake was there. He was tall and handsome and had pretty blue eyes. He was a reporter for the *Star-Ledger* and was incredibly friendly. Talking to him made me feel like a speck of ash in the street.

Her sister Eve was there. She'd finished college in May and was now a web designer at First Light Multimedia, where Craig worked, a deal I'd helped facilitate.

Their grandfather Sol was there, their mom's dad, an old-school New Yorker who'd worked in the garment business and now used a walker and gave everyone a charming hard time. Sol and I sat in the living room by the fire. He told me stories of the garment biz and what the city had been like in his day. Wait a while, he'd say as he paused to compose his next thought. Then he'd begin speaking again, eyes closed.

At dinner I sat next to Samantha's dad. He gave a heartfelt toast to family, friends, and good food during which he seemed to come close to tears. He'd grown up in Chicago and during the meal we talked about Wrigley Field. He waxed nostalgic about going to Cubs games as a kid. He asked me if I could only eat one thing for dinner for the rest of my life, what would it be? I said probably a Whopper.

Afterward everyone moved into the living room. Conversation continued. Samantha's family engaged one another and listened attentively with expressions of genuine interest. It was astonishing to me.

My family was consumed by endless squabbles, resentments, grudges. My mom hadn't spoken to one of her sisters in seven years. She talked shit about this sister to her other sister, who in turn talked shit about my mom behind her back. My five uncles were variously funny, gregarious, hostile, racist, generous, intelligent, misogynist, self-pitying, charming, and manic-depressive. My uncle Art, who had lived in our basement for two years in the mid-eighties and was at that time my only male role model, was a lying and manipulative philanderer. His unctuous way with women extended even to my own girlfriend—Erin—for whom he once purchased underwear, unbidden by her and without my knowledge. Get the whole crew in a room together and no one listened to a word you said. They talked over and around you and when they actually let you speak you could tell they were only biding their time till it was their turn to speak again. They insulted you to your face and then laughed and said they were just kidding. They battered you with the sheer brute force of their personalities.

I flashed on a Thanksgiving from my childhood: my grandfather screams at me for putting on his shoes, messes up carving the turkey, storms out of the house, drives to a bar, returns hours later blind drunk.

This was different. This felt good. I left that night wishing I was part of Samantha's family—not to get there by marriage but for it to already have been so.

There was no year-end bonus at First Investors. Instead we were given a catalog filled with dollar-store merchandise, told to select an item and jot down the corresponding order number. No payment necessary, it was all on them. I ordered a set of green nonstick cookware whose handles all bent the first time I washed them.

—Knock knock.

I turned in my chair. Clara stood over me, smiling benignly.

—Got a minute?

—Sure.

I followed her into her office. She sat and told me to close the door.

—Uh-oh. This must be serious.

She smiled and said no. She paused and composed herself.

—I think you've been working on your own writing.

—My own writing?

—Yes. Your own outside writing.

—And why do you—what makes you think that?

—There have been times when I've walked by and I've noticed other things on your screen, things that obviously aren't work-related.

—Well. That may be. But I have to say I've never worked on any of my own writing here. Even if I wanted to I wouldn't be able to.

I was telling the truth.

—All I know is what I've seen. And you know George sees these things too. He's very perceptive. And it just doesn't look good when you have non-work-related material up on your screen.

—Is there something . . . has the quality of my work fallen off or is there some other reason you think I might not be concentrating or—

—No. No it isn't that—

—Because you may have seen me on the Internet or something but I'm telling you honestly I've never worked on anything here except work.

—I just thought I'd tell you. I'm trying to help you. Your review's coming up in a few months and I wanted to give you a chance to correct some things before George and I get together and he decides your raise.

I sat looking at her. She looked at me. She had a thin bird-like face. Her hair was short and feathered. Her stare was at once genial and accusatory. I had my hands crossed in my lap to keep them from shaking.

The little plane rocked down through thick white clouds. Snow swirled at the window. When the tires hit the runway I let out a long breath. My mom and Ed picked me up at the airport. We drove along in Ed's pickup, the three of us squeezed in the cab. Snow slithered over the road, covered the fields and trees. There were no tall buildings. I couldn't see any people. Everywhere the snow was pure and white. We pulled into the driveway and eased into the garage. Our dog Lucky was looking out from the side-door window. The freezing air smelled clean and fresh.

I drove into Kalamazoo and went to Harvey's. It was mobbed. I ran into an old pal of mine, Reg.
   —Hey. How's New York?
   —Good.
   —What are you doing out there?
   —I'm a writer for a financial company on Wall Street.
   —Wall Street?
   —Yeah. Just something I sorta fell into.
   —Weird. Is Paul still out there?
   —Yeah we live together.
   —How's he doing?
   —Good.
   Reg and I went back six, seven years. We'd been close for a time. We'd spent long nights sitting on porches talking shit or listening to records or driving around Kalamazoo looking for something to do. Our bands had played shows together. We'd ridden in vans packed with our friends and our gear. We'd snarfed

late-night meals at Denny's with two, three tables full of loud punk rockers.

All this had happened but there was little to say now. I got the vibe Reg thought I thought I was a hero for blowing town and he was a chump for staying and that he maybe viewed me as a sell-out for the Wall Street shit. We stood in silence a minute longer. I indicated my empty glass and went to the bar for another drink.

Snow was falling again. A good few inches had accumulated in the time I'd been in the bar, on top of the five or so already on the ground. I drove home blitzed, took the back roads, cruised down Vine going fifteen miles an hour then merged onto Kings Highway. It was snowing so heavily I could only go twenty, twenty-five maximum. On the left was the paper mill where Ed had worked all those years and I'd worked those two summers. After that was a strip club called the Country Palace then the stoplight in Comstock then nothing but open fields and a few scattered houses till downtown Galesburg. I passed no other cars. Pavement played on the stereo. The headlights illuminated only billions of snowflakes flying at me insanely and barely discernable tire tracks in the drifts in the road.

Back in Brooklyn, 12/31/99.

We stood on our roof as the clock struck midnight. Cheers and car honks filled the neighborhood. We could see the skyline and I held my breath, wondering if any of the crackpot fantasies would come true. A computer meltdown shuts down power in the city. A dirty bomb in Times Square spews toxic clouds into the sky. But the fireworks exploded and the skyline stayed standing and we toasted the new year.

Trish had rolled into town a few days ago. She was here to stay, living in the apartment now. She was in the process of transferring to a community college in lower Manhattan. She'd whipped up platters of munchies for the small gathering, mostly Paul's friends. Around 11:50 the party had moved to the roof. Now a few minutes after the turn of the century Paul stood holding a beer yelling at the Citibank tower:

—FUCK YOU, CITIBANK! FUCK YOUR FEES! FUCK YOUR TRICKLE EFFECT!

I went into Manhattan around two a.m. A guy entered the subway car and walked from person to person shaking everyone's hand, saying Happy New Year. I got out Eighty-sixth Street and walked two blocks north to Samantha's. She'd gone to some party that cost money, some all-inclusive thing. She'd asked me to go. I told her I just couldn't see going to a party you had to pay for.

She was passed out when I arrived. Her roommate's little sister buzzed me in. I walked into Samantha's room and took off my clothes. I got in bed and closed my eyes. The room spun and dipped. I heard her next to me breathing.

What's happening now?

Trish got a job in the financial district at a breakfast-and-lunch spot called Brewbaker's, whose business entailed mostly office deliveries. She had to be at work at six a.m. but was afraid to commute that early alone. She talked Paul into getting up and driving her into the city. At first he would drop her off and then come home and sleep a while longer. Then he began working at Brewbaker's himself. He pushed a cart through the streets bringing coffee, pastries, and sandwiches to offices. One of the places he went was First Investors, which used Brewbaker's to cater occasional higher-level meetings. One day I had to attend such a meeting. I brought my pen and notepad into the conference room. There was a spread on the table—bagels, various cream cheeses, muffins, fruit. Over on the counter were two thermoses of coffee and two cartons of milk in an ice-filled bucket. I sat at the table with my notepad before me. I looked at the food my best friend had placed there just moments ago. I fixed myself a coffee and got a muffin. I put it on a napkin and sat waiting for the meeting to start.

My mother was on the phone saying she didn't know how she'd gotten herself into such a pickle so late in life.

She was talking about Happy Hearts, Inc.

It began in the late eighties when she wrote a manual on how to lower cholesterol and live a heart-healthy lifestyle. She'd been contracted to write it for the hospital she worked at but there was a regime change and my mom was laid off. After some mild negotiation and a vague legal threat, she bought the rights to the project for a dollar. Over the years Happy Hearts had evolved through various formats or ideas for formats. At one point she envisioned a phone-based system of information retrieval modeled on Ticketmaster. Now it seemed to be mostly a consulting venture, or at least that was the intent. The prized feature, according to my mom, was a test consisting of a few simple questions that apparently helped determine your risk of contracting heart disease. She'd been working on Happy Hearts with varying degrees of focus and intensity for many years. It had devoured money—Ed had footed the bill for all of it—and brought in none. Occasionally to make ends meet she took menial jobs. She'd worked at the JCPenney in the mall during the Christmas rush and as a bagger at Meijer's. Now she worked part-time at the Meijer's gas station on Gull Road.

—I've been meaning to write you a letter to try and explain.

—You don't have to do that, I said.

—I know but I want to. I've been working on this thing for half your life now.

—Half my life?

—Well since what, eighty-seven?

—Eighty-seven? I was thirteen. So, you know, not quite half my life.

She laughed. —Close enough.

—It's all right, mom.

—I would've at least liked to help pay for your college.

I had taken out student loans for college. I was twenty thousand dollars in debt. —It's all right, I said.

—You and Ed have been so patient but jeez, like I said. One day I just woke up and thirteen years had gone by.

—You never know. It could still work out.

—We'll see. I've got a couple things cookin . . .

She explained that she'd met a new potential partner. He was a sharp guy. They were in talks to see where they could go with this thing.

After hanging up I sat on the couch thinking of my mother's dreams and all the years of hard work that so far hadn't panned out. I pictured her behind the counter at a gas station ringing up someone's cigarettes and it broke my heart.

At Union Square I exited a Manhattan-bound L train. I saw Erin across the platform boarding a Brooklyn-bound train. I hesitated and the train doors closed behind her. I walked over quickly, looked through the glass and knocked. She and some other people looked up and I waved. She saw me and smiled. As the train pulled away she put up a hand and waved back.

I was lying on Samantha's bed, face buried in a pillow. She was meeting some friends at a bar in the neighborhood and asked me to come. I said no. She asked why. I said I was tired and tomorrow was a writing day. But there was another reason: I had nothing to say to her friends. They were nice but they'd all been in fraternities or sororities. They worked in marketing or finance — not as a place-holder while they pursued other ambitions but because marketing and finance were their true interests. At first I was psyched to have broken in with this crowd. In college I lusted after sorority babes from afar. Now I was having drinks with them in dark Manhattan bars. The guys in this scene were mostly finance geeks. I felt insecure in their presence and avoided speaking to them whenever possible. The women were foxy careerists—to a point. Most were obsessed, though only in their mid-twenties, with landing a mate and settling down.

Still, the main reason I begged off—the thing that now influenced virtually all my decisions—was I wanted to get some writing done.

—You could just come out for one drink, said Samantha.

—One drink is never one drink.

—Yes it is. Please. You never wanna come out.

I didn't reply.

—Is that a no?

—I wanna get up early and get going. I haven't written anything lately. I'm way off schedule.

—It'll be fun, she said.

—It's never fun.

—What's not?

—The bar. Going out to the bar. It's not fun.

—Not this again.

—What?

—Your whole thing about how there's no such thing as fun.

—I never said that.

—Yes you did.

—No. What I said was people overuse the word fun. They overstate the degree to which they enjoy things.

—Bryan come on. You have fun.

—I do. Just not at a loud bar on a Friday night.

—I bet if I wanted to go to St. Mark's bookstore you'd go.

—Maybe.

—See?

—I'm kidding. I'm in for the night.

—Okay then. I'll see you when I get back.

She was looking for a new job. She was on the phone with head-hunters constantly, speaking in a low voice in her cubicle. She began interviewing at bigger, more prestigious firms. I was sad at the thought of her leaving but I knew she wasn't happy at First Investors. I helped her write cover letters and encouraged her in her search. She came over one day and said she had something to tell me. Something she couldn't say here. We walked into the little conference room and closed the door.

—So I was talking to a headhunter about a job.

—Yeah?

—A writing job at Morgan Stanley.

—That sounds good. Are you gonna apply?

—No. It's straight writing and that's not what I'm looking for. But the way she was talking about it I thought it'd be good for you.

—Me?

—Yeah.

—I'm not looking for a job.

—I know but come on. Look around. Do you like it here?

—No. You know I don't.

—So why not apply?

—What is it again?

—It's a writing position, funds marketing. It's the same thing you do here.

—Yeah but Morgan Stanley?

—What's wrong with that?

—Nothing. I just don't wanna work eighteen hours a day.

—You're not gonna work that much, that's for bankers and analysts.

—Yeah?

—Yeah. Plus you'll be getting paid a lot more.

—How much more?

—I don't know, she didn't say.

I thought a moment.

—I read in the paper that Morgan Stanley switched to business casual.

—See? No more ties.

—Who's this person you talked to?

We spent an hour at Kinko's updating my resume. The headhunter reviewed it. She said there was a chance I was too junior for the position but she'd send it along anyway, couldn't hurt. A day or two later she called.

—Good news, Bryan. They wanna see you at Morgan Stanley.

—They do?

—Yeah. When can you do it?

—Uh. Well . . .

—What's wrong?

—Nothing.

—Do you not want the interview?

—No I do. I'm just a little surprised. I mean I wasn't even looking.

—Bryan you get Morgan on your resume, stay there a year, and trust me, you'll be able to write your own ticket. Go anywhere you want.

She called back later with the details.

—You're gonna go to Two World Trade Center and check in at the security desk. They'll call up to Ginny.

I was writing as she spoke.

—Two World Trade Center. What floor again?

—Seventy.

—Seventy. Got it.

—Good luck, Bryan. Let me know how it goes.

* * * *

Ginny met me at the front desk. I did a quick scan of the area outside her office — 5:30 and mostly empty, a promising sign. Ginny had a picture of James Dean on her wall. I'd been obsessed with Dean for a time during college and mentioned visiting Fairmount, Indiana, his hometown, just a few hours south of Kalamazoo.

She looked through my portfolio. She showed me some of the projects her team had been working on. An outside firm had designed the materials. They were large and colorful and generally hipper and more expensive-looking than my First Investors pieces. I got a good vibe from Ginny. She had friendly blue eyes. Throughout the interview I snuck peeks out the window. I'd never seen anything like the view. It was dark and clear out and there was Manhattan like an architect's model, lights spread out below bleeding north into the cluster of tall Midtown buildings — but even those looked small from up here, the Empire State building roughly the size of my pinky, the whole scene framed by purple sky and pale clouds.

— That's quite a view.

Ginny looked out and smiled.

— That's the best part of my day.

I returned a week later for two more interviews, one with a guy named Frank who had the office next to Ginny's and talked to me for maybe six minutes, the other with the head of the department, Lois. Lois was tall, nearly my height. She wore shiny pink lipstick and licked her lips constantly, frantically, to the extent that you had to concentrate to keep from staring. She asked few questions, yet still managed to keep me there for the better part of an hour. She gabbed on and on. I nodded and looked serious. I kept my eyes on her eyes and not her quickly flicking tongue.

* * * *

The offer was fifty thousand a year plus a bonus. It might as well have been a million for how I reacted—sweating and hyperventilating and delirious with good fortune.

—Way to go, kid. You did it, said my mom.

She passed the phone to Ed.

—What's this now?

—I got a new job. I'm gonna be working at Morgan Stanley.

—Hey that's great. What are they gonna be payin ya?

—Fifty thousand.

Ed whistled. —Making the big bucks now, ain't ya.

I laughed. —I guess so.

—Congratulations, Brain. I'm real prouda ya. I worked my whole life and never made more'n forty.

I went to Century 21 and Banana Republic and loaded up on business-casual gear. Black Kenneth Cole shoes with a squared-off toe. Monochromatic stretch poplin button-downs, polo shirts, slate-gray Dawson chinos. I rocked these new threads my last day at First Investors, a Casual Friday.

Good riddance, Clara, to your *knock-knock*s and the sound of you constantly cracking open Diet Pepsis and your terrible feathered hair.

Good riddance, George, to your balloon ass and your smug fucking comments and multicolored pens.

Peter and Jeff took me out for drinks after work. Peter's wife Helga met up with us. They all knew about me and Samantha, we'd told them at the start. I wasn't sure if anyone else at First Investors knew and now it wouldn't matter because we were both leaving. She'd gotten a new job the week after I had—interactive marketing at Credit Suisse. She was over the moon. She explained the new gig to me several times but I still didn't quite understand what she'd be doing.

We sat at an outside table at a bar in Tribeca. I was stoned on cocktails, grooving the whole mad scene. Steady streams of pretty people strode past our table. I was so happy I'd moved here and made such great friends and was doing this exact thing at this exact moment. I got up from the table, went to the bathroom, and pissed. I looked at myself in the mirror as I stood washing my hands.

I haven't written in so long but now I'm making all this money and working in the World Trade Center and none of it was ever my dream but it's all right too and I'm sure if I hang in there I'll figure things out and set up a new schedule and start writing again. I'll write something good and then it'll get published and then I'll be happy.

Twin Cities

Two days later I flew to Minneapolis. Bits and I walked through the airport on our way to his car. I told him there'd been a pro wrestler on the plane.

—Oh yeah? Which one?

—I don't know. Some kids were waiting at the gate to get his autograph. He had a hillbilly name. Big John or Bo Bob or some shit like that.

—How'd those kids know he was gonna be on that plane?

—Beats me. Maybe Wrestlemania's in town.

Bits laughed. —Wrestlemania.

—You know I took Daisy Landis to Wrestlemania once. Wings Stadium, ninety-two. My friend Weston took Carly. We went on a double date.

—To Wrestlemania?

—Maybe it wasn't Wrestlemania. But it was definitely big-time wrestling. It was a big fucking spectacle with all the superstars.

—Hulk Hogan?

—I don't know if he was there. I don't think he was.

—Junkyard Dog?

—I can't remember who was there now. I just remember going.

—Daisy lives here now, doesn't she?

—She does. I got in touch with her last week and told her I was coming.

—When you gonna see her?

—I don't know, I'm supposed to call.

—What's she doing these days?

—She works for Target as a buyer of some kind.

—Everyone in Minneapolis works for Target.

—You don't.

—Maybe I should. I'd make a lot more money.

We walked along. —Weird, said Bits. —I never got Daisy.

—What do you mean?

—She was always nice to me when I saw her in the halls or whatever. She just seemed, I don't know. Not that interesting to me. But I know you had a thing for Portage Northern girls. All you Gull Lake dudes did.

I laughed. —The Huskies were special.

We walked out to the parking garage and got in the car.

—So what's this new job?

—Financial writing. Same kinda thing.

—Morgan Stanley. They're a big deal, right?

—Bigger than the last place.

—How much they paying you?

—Fifty thousand.

—Fifty thousand. Shit.

—They gave me a nice bump.

—Are you still gonna be on Wall Street?

—Close. The World Trade Center.

A minute or two passed.

—Fifty Gs, said Bits. —Sweet.

Bits lived in a studio apartment in an old brick building. These were his last days of single living. Zoe was done with school and coming to Minneapolis in a few weeks. She and Bits were moving in together.

We went to the movies and saw *American Psycho* and roared at the part where Christian Bale is fucking the girl from behind while flexing his muscles and checking himself out in the mirror. We drove out to Bloomington to the Mall of America. I took pictures of the LEGO Imagination Center and the amusement park with the giant inflatable Snoopy and one of Bits with a virtual reality gizmo strapped to his face. We hung out with his bandmates and jammed at their practice space and played some old songs Bits and I had written together. I missed the feeling of playing amplified, of standing at the mic piecing together melodies over fragments of chords.

One morning we rose early and drove to Kalamazoo. The drive took ten hours. We arrived after dark. Bits stayed with Zoe. I stayed in Galesburg with my folks. My mom gushed over my new job and said how exciting it was that I was going to be working in the World Trade Center. It seemed like I could have been scrubbing toilets there and she would have been just as proud. Ed's concerns were more bottom-line. Damn, you can't beat the money, he said.

We stayed in Michigan a full day. Bits picked me up the next morning and we split. We stopped at a Hooter's outside Chicago for lunch. Somewhere in Wisconsin we stopped at a Subway for dinner. It was tucked in a bowling alley and after we ate we walked out and took in the scene. It was crowded and smoky. Pins crashed and music played. People were drinking and laughing and having fun. For a moment it made me incredibly sad and I missed the midwest more than anything. Then we got in the car and drove away.

On Friday I called Samantha at work to congratulate her on her last day at First Investors. She didn't answer. I called back later and she still didn't answer. I stood there thinking and then it hit me—her last day had been Thursday. I dialed her home number and got her answering machine. I left a message. I thought maybe she was with Eve. I tried to remember Eve's number and couldn't. I checked my e-mail. There was a message from Samantha. *Why no call?* it said.

Bits and I sat on the couch in Daisy's apartment. She sat facing us in a chair on the other side of a glass coffee table. Light poured in through a sliding glass door. Bits and Daisy spent a few minutes catching up and then conversation petered out. Dead center on the table was a bowl of Bottle Caps candies.

—You mind if I have some Bottle Caps? said Bits.

—Of course not, said Daisy.

She nudged the bowl toward us. Bits reached in.

—Bryan you want a few?

—Sure.

He handed me a package. Daisy took some. We munched Bottle Caps.

—Pretty good, I said.

—I got them free at work, said Daisy.

—Not bad, said Bits.

A few minutes later he left. Daisy and I sat there. It was still strange. She wouldn't quite meet my eye. Keys rattled at the door. Her roommate came in. Introductions were made. The roommate smiled and was cheerful.

—What are guys up to?

—Not too much, said Daisy. —We're gonna get dinner.

—Ooh where you goin?

—I don't know, we haven't figured it out yet.

They tossed around the names of a few restaurants.

—Well I'm sure you'll think of somethin, said the roommate. —Anyway don't mind me. I'm just gonna grab a few things and I'll be out of your way.

She went into her room and closed the door. She came out a while later holding a small suitcase. She explained that she was going away for the weekend and said have a good time, nice meeting you, Bryan. Then she left.

—Do you like Thai food? said Daisy.

—Thai's one of my favorites.

At the restaurant, after a few sips of wine, we loosened up. Daisy told me about work. Things were happening fast. She'd been promoted again recently and was putting in long hours. People worked under her now. She wrote performance reviews and departmental reports.

A waitress came over. We ordered pad Thai.

—How many peppers? said the waitress.

—How many what?

—How spicy, said Daisy. —Four is the hottest.

—Three peppers, I said.

The waitress left. Daisy sipped wine.

—Are you excited about you new job?

—I'm excited about the money.

—Are you still writing?

—Trying to. But no, not much. Last year I was writing poems. It was going pretty good actually and then . . .

—What?

—I don't know. You know how it is.

—You'll get back to it one day.

—Yeah you think so?

—Sure. I know you. I remember you used to write me poems.

—I remember that too. Love poems. I remember them not working.

She shook her head. —What was I thinking?

—You were thinking you dug that guy Jean Pierre.

—Jean Pierre. I forgot about him.

—I didn't, that cocksucker.

She laughed. —God, your memory.

—Do you remember our first kiss?

—Yes. It was at Mark's house.

—That's right, at Mark's house, in the upstairs closet.

—The closet?

—Yeah. The closet with all his diving suits and scuba gear.

She laughed. —Right. It's coming back to me. Why the closet again?

—I wanted it to be special. I wanted to make sure I'd remember it.

—What'd we do after that?

—After that we made out on the floor by the couch. There was, I remember there was a *Ren and Stimpy* tape playing and then the tape stopped and the glow from the TV turned the room blue.

—Meanwhile Mark and Carly were screwing like rabbits in his room.

—Probably.

—Using handcuffs or whatever.

—That sounds about right.

—See, we were innocent. All we ever did was kiss.

—Innocent? I guess you could frame it that way, yeah.

There was a pause as she picked up her glass and drank.

—You know a part of me . . . she said.

—What?

—Part of me always wished we'd . . . that we knew each other like that.

I drank some water. —Is that right?

—Maybe it's weird to say now. But it . . . it would've been nice.

—Not back then it wouldn't have, at least not on my end. It took me a while to get my game together.

She laughed. —Me too.

Another pause. —So you're, you have a girlfriend?

—I do, yeah. For almost a year now.

—How's it going?

—Good. Good. What about you. You seeing anyone?

—Yeah. We just, it's new. A couple months.

—What's he like?

—He's nice. Sweet. Much sweeter than my ex.

—What was wrong with your ex?

She ran through the list: he lacked ambition, hated her friends, was codependent, often said cruel things.

—But you were together a long time.

—Three years.

—Well there must've been something about him you liked.

—Sure. Yeah. He wasn't always like that. That was more toward the end, maybe the last year or so. And the other thing too was we had good . . .

—Yeah?

—We had a nice chemistry.

She drank some wine.

—Physical chemistry? I said.

—Yes.

I nodded as I lifted the glass to my mouth. The restaurant was crowded. Glasses clinked. People laughed politely. Voices went in and out of focus. The wine was making me warm. Daisy's apartment was empty. Her roommate wouldn't be back.

I thought of the long years leading up to this night.

We stood in her living room. The vents pumped white noise. Daisy walked past me. She picked up the phone and went into her bedroom. The door was open. I listened.

—It was good. Three peppers was really spicy tonight. No he's here. Just talking, catching up. In a few minutes. No I'm pretty tired, I'm just gonna go to bed. Okay. Okay. I will. Love you too. Bye.

She came out of the room, put the phone down, and looked at me.

—He's worried. He wanted to come over.

—That's understandable.

—I'm supposed to call when you leave.

—All right. I'll leave soon.

—Okay. Is that what you want?

I stood there. —I don't know.

—You can stay, she said. —I mean you don't have to leave right away.

—All right.

I walked past her, into her bedroom. She stood in the doorway. One of the windows was open. A breeze blew in. I thought of Samantha. Everything in the room was orderly. The bed was neatly made. I sat on it. After a minute Daisy came over and sat next to me. She took my hand. We held hands for a while and then we lay back. She put her head on my shoulder. I stared at the ceiling. The room was dark and the air was cool and Daisy felt good and I thought of Samantha.

—You probably wouldn't like me in my normal life, she said.

—Is this not your normal life?

—I mean if you knew me day to day. Maybe you wouldn't like me.

—Why do you say that?

—Because we're so different. I used to wonder why you liked me in high school. You weren't like any of the other guys who were after me. You played in a band, you wrote poetry. It made me feel good though. Special. Like you were interested in me and not just my boobs.

—Yeah. So special you dumped me.

—I didn't know what I had then.

—We were young. No one knows what they have then.

We lay there and I held her. I pulled her closer. Our hands were moving around now. I thought of Samantha. I pushed it a little further, let it go another few minutes.

—Maybe I should get going, I said.

—All right. I'll give you a ride.

She drove me to Bits's. We sat in her car and held hands.

—Well I'm glad we saw each other.

—Me too, she said.

The engine idled. A silence passed.

—I really want to kiss you, I said. —It's driving me crazy.

She leaned over and gave me a little kiss close to the lips.

—How about one more?

She kissed me again.

—Maybe we should have sex.

She laughed. —We'll see each other again soon. I'll be in New York for work. They send me there two or three times a year. We'll stay in touch.

Inside Bits was watching TV.

—How'd it go?

—All right.

—Yeah? What'd you do?

—We went to a Thai restaurant downtown and then back to her place.

—Her place, huh?

—Nothing happened.

—You have any more Bottle Caps?

I laughed. —No.

On the screen several intense British men were speaking in some code I couldn't follow. Their chat was touched with weird acid-trip visuals.

—What the fuck is this?

—*The Prisoner.* You ever seen it?

—No.

—Oh it's the best. It's about this guy who gets kidnapped and held hostage in a place called the Village. That guy there. Number Six.

—Number Six?

—Yeah. You never learn his real name. The way it starts out, he's this spy who quits his job. He goes back to his place to get some things and gets gassed and wakes up in the Village. These people interrogate him about why he resigned.

—Why did he?

—He never tells them.

—Why not?

—Because, man. He's Number Six.

The Village—the prison—was a sinister seaside resort. Number Six was told by his captors to submit. He was told to conform. He was pressed relentlessly for information but he resisted. He tried to escape the Village but couldn't. They tried to fuck with his mind but they couldn't. He told them he was not a number, he was a free man, a person. They laughed. There were other prisoners in the Village. Whenever anyone tried to escape a floating white blob rolled up out of nowhere and trapped them.

Bits stopped the tape. We got ready for bed. I turned on the fan and lay down on the eggshell foam on the floor. Bits turned out the light. We lay there a moment.

—What was up with those Bottle Caps? he said.

The South Tower

The clock radio alarm went off at 6:40. I listened to Howard Stern for a few minutes then got out of bed. I made coffee and showered and drank the coffee as I dressed. I sat on the bed wondering whether or not I was going to shit. I don't like to leave my apartment for the day without first taking a good shit. I got up and danced around a little, trying to loosen things up. Nothing happened. I watched the clock till it said exactly 7:21 and then left.

On the bus to the L train something clicked in my bowels. It skipped the lesser stages of urgency and shot straight to code red. I looked out the window. We'd just turned on Lorimer and were going by the track at McCarren Park. The bus seat vibrated steadily, mixing a terrible cocktail inside me. Occasionally we bounced through a pothole and I squeezed extra tight. Sweat broke out on my upper lip. I wiped it away. I closed my eyes and took deep breaths. My asshole was sweating, my armpits, my palms.

At last we reached Metropolitan. I got off the bus, walked to Kellogg's Diner and went in. A sign on the bathroom door said OUT OF SERVICE. I turned to the counter guy. He stared back at me pitilessly. I walked outside and stood on the sidewalk wondering what to do next. The pain subsided. I thought I might be all right. I went into the subway and waited. I stared at a blackened smear of gum on the platform, never averting my gaze. When the train came it was packed. Any other day I would've waited for the next one but time was of the essence here and I shoved my way in. We moved into the tunnel under the East River.

At First Avenue the pain returned. I knew I'd have to take action. I got off the train at Union Square and left the station. I stood on the southwest corner of Fourteenth Street and Fourth Avenue. The Virgin Megastore was closed, as was, I assumed, the Barnes & Noble on the north side of the park. There was an Au Bon Pain across the street. I set off for it with the single-minded focus of the Terminator, not knowing if they had a public restroom, not caring. I'd give them twenty dollars to use the toilet. Forty.

Fuck it—I'd give them everything in my wallet.

I walked past the line to a hallway in back. There was a restroom. I reached for the door handle thinking, oh my god please.

The door was unlocked. I went in. Shit streamed from my ass before skin touched seat. It poured out of me and it was wonderful. The restroom was pleasant—warm from the baking ovens, rich with the smell of coffee and cinnamon. When it was over I felt calm, centered. I couldn't remember feeling better in my life. The water from the faucet was hot and there was plenty of soap.

I left without buying anything and walked back to the train. The 4 came quickly and took me downtown. I got out at Fulton Street. The World Trade Center was there. The towers rose into the blue morning sky. I walked toward them.

Five World Trade Center was the squat low-rise structure on the northeast side of the complex. Morgan Stanley had several administrative floors there. I sat in a conference room with the other new hires. Representatives from various departments came in and went over the many company policies. They guided us through a packet and waited while we filled out the forms. They took us by rows to be fingerprinted. I went into a little room and a man pressed my fingers to the ink pad and rolled them over the paper. He worked quickly and gave me a wet nap when it was done.

In another little room under one of the towers I got my ID photos taken. There were two cards, one for Morgan Stanley and one for the trade center generally that unlocked the turnstiles at the elevator banks. I took these cards and walked through the lobby. It was almost noon when I clicked through the turnstile. I got into one of the big cattle-car elevators. It took me express to the skylobby on the forty-fourth floor. There the doors opened on dozens of people rushing around, many of them carrying lunches in fold-out cardboard boxes. Men in corporate security suits stared impassively as elevators dinged nonstop all around them. On forty-four there were several other elevator banks that delivered people to the higher floors. I walked to the second bank, got in another elevator, and went up to seventy.

Ginny looked at me as if she didn't know me and was trying to place me. She walked out of her office. A second later I followed. She'd stopped directly outside.

—Here's your office, she said.

But it wasn't an office, it was a cubicle. For some reason it embarrassed me that she used that word.

It was nicer and more spacious than my cubicle at First Investors. It was long and narrow, with the computer at the end. The keyboard sat on an adjustable riser attached to the desk. To the right of the computer was a printer. The desk and cabinets were a dark red wood instead of gray metal. A large tear-away calendar was centered on the desk. To the left of the desk was a visitor's chair. The cubicle walls were high but standing as I was I could see over everything to the other side of the floor.

I stepped into my new cubicle, set my coat and bag on the chair.

We took an elevator to forty-four then rode an escalator down one flight to the cafeteria. I was with Milton and Doreen, the other writers on my team. Milton was a huge man—taller than me by a good three or four inches and sixty or seventy pounds heavier, maybe more. His hand enveloped mine completely when we shook. He wore a suit despite the new business-casual dress code. Doreen was bottle-blonde and soft-spoken. We sat by a window with a panoramic view of New Jersey. They asked me questions about where I'd been previously and what I'd been doing. I answered and asked them other things back. Both had been at Morgan Stanley about a year and they both liked it. They assured me that I'd like it too. Marketing was a priority here but the workload was reasonable. There were no late nights. The company was pouring money into mutual fund materials and they looked great. If you were lead writer on a new fund or a theme brochure there was even an element of creative freedom involved.

Milton was chatty. He riffed on everyone in the department, couching his language in ways that essentially revealed his often negative appraisals. Ginny's weird, he said, distant. But don't take it personally, it took me a while to get her. She's been happier recently, you should've seen her in the midst of her divorce. Then there's Charlotte. Charlotte's, well . . .

He tilted his head, stuck his nose in the air.

Milton cracked himself up. He couldn't get through three words without laughing. He had a high good-natured chuckle that reminded me instantly of Dr. Hibbert from *The Simpsons*. He did impressions of people I hadn't yet laid eyes on, punctuating each bit with his Dr. Hibbert laugh.

—You're terrible, said Doreen. But she laughed along and occasionally chimed in with observations of her own. Then they'd pause and Milton would compose himself.

—No but it's a good group, he'd say.

That night I put a change of clothes in my backpack and returned to the city. Samantha and Eve and I went to a sushi place on Third Avenue. Eve had started a new job today too. We ordered sake and toasted our first days. Samantha was wild about her new colleagues. She said already it was clear she'd made the right move, First Investors was in the Stone Ages, she couldn't believe she'd stayed for so long. Clara and George were a sick joke, her new bosses were sharp, the projects were large and forward-thinking in scope. It was going to be a lot of work but she was ready to dive in.

After a brief, unhappy stint at First Light Multimedia Eve was now a web designer at Women.com. I asked how her first day went. Better than First Light, she said, but still just a job.

In some ways I had more in common with Eve than I did with Samantha. Eve was a painter. We liked the same music, had the same sense of humor, and were generally anxious people scared of many of the same things. She sometimes came unglued in crowds, couldn't fly without Xanax.

We drank some more. I wolfed a seaweed salad and rolls and was feeling so magnanimous I picked up the check. We left the restaurant and walked Eve to the subway. Samantha and I went to her place and trudged up the six flights.

Half an hour later we were in bed. Samantha set the alarm and switched off the table lamp. Once we'd settled in the only sounds were the traffic noise on Lexington and her roommate watching TV too loudly in the other room. We didn't get close to each other or touch. In a little while we fell asleep.

* * * *

Ginny ignored me for most of the first week. Late in the week she brought me a stack of brochures. She told me that reading them would give me a sense of the Morgan Stanley house style. I read the brochures then came back from lunch and read them again. I thought Ginny would come by and talk to me about them but she didn't. So I just kept rereading them. I always had at least one—and often two or more—folded open on my desk. I had a fresh legal pad and jotted down notes, copying statistics, percentages, and headlines from the charts.

Friday night I sat in a loud crowded bar on the Lower East Side, nursing a gin and tonic and waiting for Samantha. She was thirty minutes late. The bar had an open facade. I watched the action on the street. The last few days had been unseasonably warm. Already the women were showing more skin. That's a glorious time in the city, those first warm days, when the coats and sweaters come off and the legs and cleavage appear.

A cab pulled up. Samantha got out. She rushed into the bar and said she was sorry before she'd even reached me.

—I was getting ready to go without you, I said.

—Sorry, she said again, touching my arm. —I got here as soon as I could.

—They've got you working late on a Friday already?

—I told you. It's not like First Investors. We actually have projects to push through. I'm lucky if I get ten minutes for lunch at my desk.

I hadn't seen her since the night at the sushi place, almost two weeks ago now. Right away she'd worked late every evening. Whenever we talked she seemed tired and distracted, reluctant to make plans. If I questioned her reticence she said don't worry, it's not you, everything's fine, it's just this new job is way more demanding and I'm trying to do good.

The bartender brought her a Stoli and soda. She apologized again and asked if I was excited for tonight. I really wasn't but said yes anyway and we drank.

The reading was part of the first *New Yorker* Festival. It took place at an old synagogue that had been converted into an arts space. It was a grand and beautiful old structure with high arched ceilings, a gold-leaf altar, and a wraparound balcony. There was a podium on the altar. Rows of folding chairs were arranged on the floor. In the back on a table was a makeshift bar. We bought cocktails in plastic cups and took two seats on the aisle about halfway back. The place filled up quickly. A woman came to the podium and introduced Alice Munro, who appeared on the altar to ecstatic applause. She thanked the crowd with a disarmingly warm and beautiful smile. She seemed truly awed by the fuss. I wasn't a fan of Munro but was moved by her smile and sweet manner. My mind was open as she started to read one of her stories.

Half an hour later she was still reading but I'd checked out long ago and her voice was a drone. When she finished the room broke into more huge applause. A young woman appeared and began talking about Richard Ford. It took me a moment to grasp that she was a fiction editor at the *New Yorker*. She looked about twenty-three.

Richard Ford took the stage and explained that he would be reading two stories, one by John Cheever and one he'd written that was influenced by the Cheever piece, both called "Reunion." The Cheever story was about a boy who meets his estranged father in Grand Central. They only have an hour and a half together and they're supposed to have lunch but the dad throws alcoholic tantrums at various restaurants till finally they give up and the kid boards his train. Ford's own story was also about an encounter in Grand Central. A guy walking through at rush hour sees the husband of a woman he once had an affair with. The affair is described briefly, the men have a charged but still pretty mild exchange and then go their separate ways and that's that. Neither story really killed me. Maybe it's the drinks, I thought.

After the reading I approached Richard Ford. I had my copy of *The Sportswriter* and waited to have it signed. A film crew hovered nearby. They had a camera and a boom mic and were getting in close on every exchange. My hands were shaking as I gave him the book. The bright lights of the camera were on us. I told him I enjoyed the reading and that I was a big fan. I wanted to say more. I wanted to tell him his books had been important to me, that I'd read them at a crucial time, when I was just figuring out what it would take to try and be a writer. I wanted to tell him about finding *Rock Springs* at a book table on Astor Place shortly after moving to the city and how the stories had moved me deeply and I thought it was his best book.

I wanted to say all this. Instead I said I was a fan.

Samantha and I walked out into the warm night. We stood on the corner of Houston and Norfolk. We made vague plans to meet up the next day, before I went to another *New Yorker* Festival function. I went to kiss her but it was strange. We both seemed far away. Maybe we were tired, stressed out from the long week. We got in cabs going in opposite directions.

The next day I found her lying with her eyes closed in her usual spot on the Great Lawn. I lay down on the sheet next to her. It was another hot humid day. I was sweating and uncomfortable in dark blue jeans and a green polo. We talked a little but our conversation was forced like so many others we'd had recently. The sun beat down. I was hot and miserable. Samantha looked at me. She smiled in a strained way, one hand shielding her eyes from the sun. I gave her a kiss, got up and walked out of the park. It was a long time before I saw her again.

The panel event was at a Midtown bar called Float. The subject was Young Writers Publishing Their First Books. Float was cool and dark and smelled of stale beer. In the back was a brightly lit stage with a row of four director's chairs on it and another one off to the side. Once the crowd was settled a woman came out and sat in the fifth chair. Unfortunately Dave Eggers can't make it, she said, he's attending a wedding, in his absence we've asked another of our favorite young writers to be here, Tony Earley.

She said a bit about Earley and his books, a collection of stories and a just-published novel. Then she introduced the other writers: Matthew Klam, Zadie Smith, Aleksandar Hemon. They all came out and the discussion began.

Quickly I realized coming here was a mistake.

Listening to these people talk I didn't feel like a writer. I felt like an outsider with an impossible dream. Just another geek with his face pressed to the glass.

Hemon had come to the US from Sarajevo in 1992 with only a basic command of English. He'd been writing in the language only since 1995. I suppose you could argue this made him the ultimate outsider. Yet by my reasoning he still had the advantage, since Sarajevo was war-torn and therefore automatically sexy to editors.

Being from Michigan, on the other hand—and not even somewhere infamous like Detroit—felt like being from nowhere.

At the moderator's prompting Matthew Klam shared an anecdote about having the first short story he'd written accepted for publication by the *New Yorker*.

—The story was out with other magazines at the time and I had to call everyone else and be like . . . *sorry*, he said to much smug laughter.

But it was Zadie Smith who made me feel the worst. She was a year younger than me, first of all, and second of all was a stone fox. *White Teeth* had just been published to wild acclaim but she seemed embarrassed to have written it and went out of her way to characterize it as an immature and inferior work. She complained about what a drag the attention was, how she had to go to photo shoots now and her toes never fit right in the Prada shoes they made her wear.

— People are always saying how writing is so difficult, she said, —but when you've got *nothing else to do* . . .

I sat in the crowd in the dark thinking, shit, I wish I had fucking nothing else to do. I wish I didn't have to get up and go to my job every morning. I wish I could stay home every day and just write.

Tony Earley was the easiest for me to relate to. He seemed like a nice humble guy. But even his niceness was complicated in my mind by the fact that he'd been named one of America's best young novelists by *Granta* magazine in 1996—four years before he'd published his first novel.

The discussion ended. I went to the bathroom. When I returned people were milling around having drinks at the bar. Zadie Smith was there. I thought of going up to her but didn't know what to say. As I watched she put a cigarette to her beautiful lips. A man standing next to her eagerly held up a light.

Ginny came to my cubicle and asked if I wanted to go to lunch. For a moment I was thrown, thinking she meant just the two of us. Then she said she'd heard talk that everyone might go to Zams.

We went to the hallway and waited. No one came. We walked to the elevators. There was no one there either. We waited a few minutes. Charlotte came through the glass doors. She asked if we were going to Zams. Ginny said she'd heard we were. I looked at Charlotte. She had thin lips, a wide forehead, brown hair. Sometimes she appeared to have very nice tits, full and round. Other times they looked rather flat. Trick of the bra, I supposed. Whelan arrived. Whelan sat in the cubicle next to mine. So far we'd said nothing to each other except good morning and good night.

Ginny asked who we were still waiting on. As soon as she spoke Frank and Patrick arrived. They were mid-conversation but Frank broke off to tell us Jenny and Lila were coming, as was Stuart the temp. A moment later they were all among us, talking excitedly about Zams. Stuart asked Ginny whether or not Milton had heard. Frank wondered if maybe someone should tell Lois or Shirley. No, it was decided, let's just go.

We took the elevators down and walked outside. We crossed Church Street and went through Liberty Plaza. Dozens of people sat hunched on benches eating food from the lunch carts. The air smelled of sun and the river and spiced meat. On Broadway we took a right and walked toward Battery Park. At Trinity Church we crossed to the east side of the street. Far down I saw tourists gathered around the Wall Street bull. I knew some joker was probably standing behind it, pointing at its big bronze nuts while his buddy snapped pictures. We came to a guy in a yellow Zams T-shirt holding a tray, giving away free samples. We gathered around him. I looked at the tray. There were little strips of sandwiches with toothpicks sticking out of them. I took one and ate it. Jenny asked what I thought. Not bad, I said. She said I could get fries. I said that didn't seem exceptional. On my sandwich, she meant, I could get fries on my sandwich.

It was a narrow establishment with just a few tables. I got the grilled chicken sandwich with cheese and fries and a kiwi-strawberry Snapple. It took a while for everyone to get through the line. At last we all had our Zams. We stood on the sidewalk. Someone suggested we go eat in Battery Park. The park was crowded. The group broke up. I sat on a bench next to Stuart the temp. I'd met Stuart but hadn't talked to him much. I'd heard him in meetings dropping the names of various celebrities he'd gone to high school with in LA. He was always doing a Mr. Burns impression, wiggling his fingers together and saying *ehhxcellent*.

—Are you a writer? he asked.

—Hmm?

—I mean here. You're a writer?

—Yeah. But also I guess in the real world too. Trying to be.

—What do you write?

—Short stories. Mostly stories and poems.

—Interesting. My second cousin's a novelist. Davis Schroeder.

He mentioned a few titles. I stared at him. He asked where I wrote.

—Where? Just . . . in my apartment.

—See I'm the opposite. I like to write in cafes. I like to be out among people. I'll take my laptop to a cafe, get a coffee, and just . . .

He trailed off.

—What do you write? I said.

—Oh everything. Novels. Screenplays.

—Novels? I said. —Plural?

—Oh yeah. Definitely. I like to work on a few things at once. You know we have another writer in my family too. My grandfather.

I waited a beat before asking about his grandfather. He said the name but it wasn't familiar. He said his grandfather had written the screenplay for a famous movie from the sixties I'd seen several times. I expressed no interest and asked no follow-up questions. We ate in silence after that. Tourists and office people on lunch break walked by. Vendors sold T-shirts and snow globes and framed photos of famous New York scenes, the trade center, Wall Street, snowy Central Park. Very black men wandered through with sheets bulging with fake Rolexes and fake Louis Vuitton bags. There was a woman on a pedestal dressed like the Statue of Liberty, standing as still as the real thing. Her robes and skin were painted sparkly green, as was the box on the ground next to her into which tourists dropped cash.

Most of the projects I worked on required little more than updating existing materials with new performance information. The first phase of this process took less than an hour. I'd photocopy the brochure in question, cross out the old numbers, and write in the new data, supplied by a team of numbers-crunchers in sales. I'd fax the edits to the designers and they'd e-mail me a new document, at which point I'd double check the changes and send it around for distribution. There were thirty or so names on the distribution list but only two mattered, legal and compliance, and usually they were the only two people who responded. Once all the edits had been made and I'd received the proper sign-offs I'd get the proofs from the designer, give them a final read, and call or e-mail them back, either to make a last-minute change or tell them it was good, go to print.

Paul and Trish had moved out and left town for the summer. It happened suddenly. They'd gotten jobs at a marketing company called Youth Stream and were traveling the country promoting a new video game. Samantha had dumped me.

This job and this cubicle were all I had left.

I was lying on my bed, still in my work clothes, staring at the ceiling. I was lonely and depressed and thinking of Samantha. I missed her and hated her in equal measure. Sometimes I'd go into Manhattan and walk the streets, playing the Afghan Whigs' *1965* in my Discman, imagining I saw Samantha everywhere.

I closed my eyes. My mind roamed.

Samantha . . . Minneapolis . . . Daisy Landis . . . Daisy's room, the open window, we're on her bed, we lay back, I pull her close, feel her next to me.

The set-up at Daisy's had exceeded my fantasies—strange city, sterile yet comforting apartment, boyfriend dispatched with a lie within earshot. But I had held back—because of Samantha. She knew I'd planned to see Daisy and had amped up the sweetness, sent an e-mail saying how much she missed me. Guilt quashed my boner for Daisy. I returned to New York. Samantha cut me loose three weeks later.

Not fucking Daisy had assumed life's-regret status.

I picked up the phone and dialed information. I got the main corporate number for Target. An operator answered.

—Could you connect me with Daisy Landis, please?

—Landis . . . one moment.

The line rang. She picked up.

—This is Daisy.

—It's Bryan Charles.

—Oh. Nervous laughter. —How are you?

—All right. How are you?

—I'm good. I'm just—working.

We exchanged pleasantries. Daisy was hesitant, too formal. It annoyed me. My heart raced. I pressed on.

—I've been thinking about that time I was there in April, that night in your room. I was thinking how there was this crazy feeling between us, all this sexual tension . . .

She said nothing. I continued.

—And not only that but a kind of closeness that comes just from knowing someone so long, even if you're not always in touch, I mean I was sixteen when we met, almost ten years ago now, and I wanted you so bad then but I didn't know what to do with a girl, and I remember, when we were having dinner you said you weren't at your peak either or not in your prime or however you put it, and then out of nowhere we had this weird second chance, but for various reasons you know the timing was off or we were in relationships, I mean I'm not anymore but you probably are still. Are you?

—I am, said Daisy.

—That's—no that's good. But still. I was thinking.

Silence.

—Are you there?

—Yeah. I'm here.

She sounded distracted, vaguely concerned.

—I was thinking we could have an affair. We could recapture that moment, that feeling from that night in your room, we could get it back and make it last. We could do it forever. No matter what happens. You get married, I get married, you have kids, whatever. We see each other somehow, whenever it works out. We wouldn't tell anyone, we'd be the only ones who knew. A lifelong affair. What do you think?

—It sounds . . . it sounds nice.

—Nice? So we'll do it, we'll have a lifelong affair?

She paused. —Um. Okay, she said.

A lifelong affair? The idea was preposterous. Yet I truly wanted it. I believed all my bullshit. Give me old moments back. Let me live out of time. Shoot me a little something for these troubles, the endless sameness of days.

I saw the scene then from a sudden remove. I saw an exhausted and embittered corporate copywriter lying on a bed in rumpled business-casual clothes, talking to a woman he'd dated for three months in high school, now a stressed-out middle manager sitting in an office in Minnesota.

—I should probably get back to work, said Daisy.

—Okay. Well. Think about it.

We were all in the conference room. Every seat at the table was taken. Some people were standing leaning against the wall. Lois stood at the head of the table by a whiteboard. She wore a bright blue suit and was licking her lips. In the center of the table was a domed phone console. Occasionally someone on the other end of the line would sniff or clear their throat. Everyone was talking over everyone else. Now and then Lois would write something on the board then circle it, underline it, draw arrows pointing to it. Then Max got up and started writing things too. His team was in charge of writing the materials for this yet-to-be-named fund, which had something to do with technology. Unlimited opportunity in cutting edge sectors in the new millennium seemed to be a theme. The conference room was on the northeast corner of the building. I stared through the windows at Midtown, the Brooklyn Bridge, the East River.

All around me the chattering continued. There were more phrases on the board, more circles, more arrows, more questions, answers, dilemmas, solutions. I could hear everyone's voices but they sounded far off now, like I was hearing them through a wall. A drop of cold sweat rolled down my rib cage. Then another and another. I left the conference room and went to the men's room. I washed my hands and stared into the mirror at the young man standing there wearing slate-gray chinos and a pink stretch button-down.

My chest was tight. I took deep breaths. I went into the farthest stall, the handicapped stall, the most spacious stall with the highest toilet. I took down my pants and sat waiting for this strange feeling to pass. I wiped out my armpits and put folded toilet paper under each arm.

Back in the meeting everyone was still talking. A moment later there was a knock at the door. It was Mr. Wallace, the security guard, saying the food had arrived. Lois had ordered lunch from Au Mandarin, the expensive Chinese place over in the World Financial Center. Plates were passed around and white plastic containers filled with glistening concoctions, cans of Coke, bottled water. Everyone kept talking around the food in their mouths. I ate with my arms down so the toilet paper wouldn't fall out.

Reunions

Erin lived now on Graham Avenue just south of Metropolitan, in an apartment over a deli with mint-green siding. Her roommate Thad played in Fake French Accent, Remington's band, and wore skin-tight jeans pegged at the ankle. On the phone she'd told me he put a big furry hat on every morning and left it on for a few minutes to get his hair properly mussed before going to work. We were in her room. There was a desk with a mirror and a curling iron and some other things on it. A TV on a table at the foot of her bed.

We'd talked more or less easily on the phone. We stood in silence now. Thad was in the other room playing a Fender Mustang through an effects board. Erin smiled and nodded. I went over and hugged her. A moment later she returned my embrace.

—I'm sorry, I said again.

We went up to her roof and sat looking out at the neighborhood. She asked about Samantha. I told her the truth—there'd been a long slow phase-out and then she dumped me over the phone.

—Over the phone?

—Yes.

—What is she, in middle school?

—I don't know. Maybe. She's seeing someone else now.

—How do you know?

—Because I called her and asked her.

—And she told you?

—No. She said what's that got to do with anything.

—Which means yes.

—Exactly.

—What did you say?

—I hung up.

—Classic Bryan.

Erin had switched jobs. She now worked days at a club called Lava. She'd dated here and there, nothing serious. She was still friends with all the old gang.

—You motherfucker, she said.

—What?

—I told myself I wasn't ever going talk to you again. I really did. I cried and was sad for a while. But then I got over it and said never again.

—Yeah but you couldn't handle it. You thought of me constantly.

She laughed. —I really didn't.

Then in early July my mom came to town. I met her after work at a Midtown office where she'd gone to see a venture capitalist to ask for money for Happy Hearts. We took the 6 downtown and walked to a beautiful old townhouse on Gramercy Park. It was a private club of some kind, somewhat musty inside but interesting to look at, like being in a museum. Her college friend Patricia was waiting at the bar. We ordered drinks. My mom and Patricia talked and laughed loudly in the big empty room. I nursed a gin and tonic and stood listening. Patricia talked with pride about the club. It was quite renowned, she assured us. A number of prominent actors of both stage and screen had been members over the years. She mentioned some names. She lit a cigarette. I moved away from the smoke. Actors? I didn't get it. It was my understanding that Patricia worked for a trade magazine, something to do with textiles. My mom looked around, marveling at the interiors. Wouldn't it be fun if I was a member, she said.

—Me?

—Yeah. Think of all the people you'd meet here, talented people. And the contacts you'd make, I mean . . . *whoa.*

I smiled tightly and looked into my drink.

—Patricia would sponsor you, wouldn't you, Patricia?

Patricia blew smoke and smiled grimly through the haze. Someone entered the room. Patricia smiled and waved.

—Garvey darling. Come. You must meet my friends.

A man with sallow skin and white hair walked over. He was smoking. He wore a striped linen suit. They kissed on the cheek. Introductions were made. Patricia spoke of Garvey's many achievements on the stage. He listened, chuckled dryly. He reminisced for a while in a low deep smoker's voice. He had a faintly British accent. My mom appeared to be spellbound.

—That *voice,* she kept saying. —*Ah.*

—Isn't it wonderful, said Patricia.

—Your voice, said my mother to Garvey.

Garvey grinned. His lips were dry, his teeth. Smoke floated up from the cigarette in his dry-looking hand. He leaned close to my mother and whispered something in her ear. She put her hand to her neck and smiled as if he'd uttered wonderful things.

—Well, she said, —my *dear.*

Another man came over. His name was Vonroy. Everyone began talking. Patricia suggested we get another drink and go out on the balcony, it was lovely out there. She had smoke in her mouth and her voice was thick with it and little puffs seeped out with each word.

* * * *

Out on the balcony I drank another gin and tonic and stared at Gramercy Park, locked away forever behind its severe iron fence. Patricia saw me looking and said club members had access to a key. I said I'd never been inside before and maybe I could go over there now. She said she'd check and see. I heard my name. My mom grabbed my arm and pulled me over to where she was standing with Vonroy.

—My son wrote a play once. Bryan tell him about your play.

—What?

—I was talking to Vonroy and he said he's a playwright. And I thought of that play that you wrote. What was the name of it? The one you wrote in college? The one you won a prize for? Oh come on, you know, the one where they're in a dirty bookstore?

She turned to Vonroy.

—Oh but it's not what you think. That's just the setting. Trust me. My son may be warped but he *is* talented.

She laughed. I grinned.

—No but really, she said. —It's a great play.

—Oh? said Vonroy.

—Oh yes. It won a prize.

She meant the undergraduate creative writing awards. I'd won the playwriting category my last year at Western. The English department held a ceremony at the top of Sprau Tower. I was given a paper certificate. My mom still talked about it as if I'd won the Pulitzer.

—Vonroy could read your play. He could give you some pointers. He could show it to some of the people he works with. Would you do that?

Vonroy hesitated. —Well. Sure.

She turned to me, smiling. —See, Bry?

—Yes.

—What's the best way for him to get it to you?

—Here. Here is the best place. Why not send it here?

He lingered another moment before moving away. I went to the end of the balcony and stood alone, finishing my drink.

The next day my mom took a cab to the World Trade Center. We stood in the conference room looking out at the city. The office had cleared out, most people had left for the holiday. I heard the shush of feet on the carpet. Patrick came in. I introduced him to my mom and he came along on our tour. They talked about California, where they'd both grown up. We went around to the conference rooms on all four corners of the building, taking in the views. It was a clear sunny day. We could see for many miles. Through the south-facing windows was the harbor, the tall ships there for the Fourth of July.

Patrick split. My mom and I took the subway to Houston Street and headed east. We stopped at Katz's and ordered pastrami sandwiches. As we were eating she told me again I should send my play to Vonroy.

—Mom.

—He could help you. You could be missing out on a great opportunity.

—Mom. I'm not doing it. Stop bringing it up.

A little white-haired man wearing big sunglasses came over and asked if we'd like more pickles. My mom said yes. The man called to a server, who delivered a large bowl of them. The man stood at our table gabbing, flirting with my mom. He said he was part owner of the place. He saw my disposable camera and said we could get a picture with him if we wanted. I started to say no that's okay but my mom said sure. The man pulled us from our seats and spoke to another server, this time requesting a couple of sausages. The server brought two huge sausages and gave one to me and one to my mom. The man put his arms around both our waists and pulled us close. I towered over him. He held me tightly. The person who brought the sausages took the picture. I was horrified but smiled anyway, holding that big sausage aloft.

—Be sure and bring me a copy, said the man, —I'll put it up on the wall. See you later, sweetheart, he said to my mom.

Over in the next cubicle Whelan was arguing with his wife again, speaking on the phone in harsh hushed tones. These days they argued constantly. They were going through hard times. Listening to Whelan explain things to his father I learned there'd been hard times previously and that his wife had gone back to Germany briefly, where she was from.

After a while I felt strange listening and got up from my desk. I did a tour of the office. I took the elevators down and walked through the mall. I stopped at Borders and looked at the new-release table, checking author bios for birth years and schools. I went outside and sat on a bench on the plaza. I looked at the people and the fountain with the big gold sphere.

Back on seventy I stopped by Dana's cubicle. On her desk was a picture of her and her boyfriend in the lobby of the Empire State building. His name was Jake. They were getting married in the fall. In the office behind us Sylvia talked on the phone, laughing her high-pitched maniacal laugh.

—How do you stand it? I said.

—What?

—Her. She sounds like fucking Beaker from the Muppets.

Dana laughed. —Bryan. You're bad.

I walked to my desk and checked my e-mail. There were several new messages but none that pertained directly to me. I stared into the computer. The hours crawled.

We were sitting next to each other on her bed. I was wearing my work clothes. The lights were off but I could still see her clearly. She lifted her shirt. I stared at her breasts in the glow from the streetlight. I sat up and kissed her. We fell back on the bed. I took off my shirt. She sat up still kissing me. I pulled off her shirt. Her hair spilled down and fell around her shoulders. Erin lay back and I lay on top of her and felt warm skin on skin. Later we lay watching television, talking and joking, saying it had to happen, it was bound to happen. We didn't say anything about it being the last time.

Saturday morning I woke late. I made coffee and ate breakfast and watched some TV. I listened to music and thumbed through some books and looked out the window and played guitar. Finally I walked to the back room and sat at my desk. I turned on my computer, opened a blank Word document, and stared at the blinking cursor without a thought in my head. I wrote for a while, stopped and read the lines. I read them over and over and then highlighted and deleted them and started again. After a while I stopped and deleted that too. I went to the kitchen for a glass of water and came back. I looked at the tree outside my window then back at the screen. I typed some words and then stared at the tree again. It was hemmed in by power lines. A black plastic shopping bag was trapped in the branches. It had been there so long it was faded and full of holes. I'd first noticed it during the winter when the branches were bare and now the leaves had grown in around it. I thought of trying to free it but couldn't figure out how. Lean out the window with a broom handle, maybe? Throw something over there? The bag snapped and fluttered in the breeze. How could I be expected to concentrate with that snapping? I looked at the computer. A car with a booming system drove by. It stopped at the light at the end of the block and the whole frame shook and rattled with the bass line. Then it went through the light and was gone. In the next apartment someone walked from the back room to the kitchen, the kitchen to the back room. Across the street a kid was yelling for Anthony to come out. I deleted what was on the screen and shut down my computer. I took a shower and left the apartment.

Mattie sat in my cubicle telling me the story of the bombing. I'd met Mattie before but didn't know her well. She always seemed sort of scattered, popping in and out of meetings, proclaiming how busy she was, never lingering. Yet here she was now, telling me the story of the bombing.

She said most people in the department were new but she and Ginny and a few others were here in '93 and were working the day the truck bomb went off in the parking garage and they walked down in the dark and smoky stairwell and it had taken them hours to get out.

She said it was funny too because Max was out on press that day and as time went on they could tell he was sort of mad that he missed it, a little jealous, and even to this day, she said, Max got a little peeved whenever anyone brought it up because in his mind they shared a bond from which he was forever excluded.

She said a few weeks later she came back to grab some files and had to have a police escort and it was, god it was eerie, her desk was just the way she'd left it, half a moldy bagel on her desk, papers spread out like she'd only just gone to the bathroom or something.

Sometime later I asked Ginny about the bombing. She shared her recollections and told me that when they finally reopened the building there was a coffee cup waiting on everyone's desk with a picture of the twin towers on it and the words WELCOME BACK.

At a party at a bar on Avenue A I met a woman named Hasna. She wore dark jeans, a dark long-sleeve shirt, and a dark head scarf that showed only her face, the skin of which was quite pale and smooth. She had a great smile and laughed easily. I sat next to her at the end of the bar and we talked.

She was from Detroit. I was blown away. I loved meeting people from Michigan. She knew what Meijer's was. She knew that *soda* was actually *pop*. She'd been to Kalamazoo to see rock shows and even knew the names of a couple of my old pals. She was twenty-two and liked Dischord and Touch and Go bands. She worked various freelance fact-checking and copy-editing jobs. She'd worked at some public-policy journal and now worked at *Rolling Stone*.

As we sat there I studied her. I was intrigued.

She's drinking Cokes, not alcohol, and wearing the scarf. These must be religious deals—or the scarf is at least. Then again she likes Fugazi so maybe she's straight edge and that's why she doesn't drink. And if she *is* religious, isn't it against the rules to even be in a bar? To wear jeans? Doesn't it have to be a long skirt?

Who was I kidding—I didn't know about any of this. I was ignorant of most of the world's cultures. I wasn't even sure what religion I meant. But there was something about her. I liked her immensely.

She mentioned a Guided by Voices show she was going to, a private show at the Bowery Ballroom next week. A friend of hers said he'd put her on the guest list. He was managing the opening band. I'm jealous, I said, I love GBV. She said I could go in her place if I wanted. She didn't know much about GBV anyway. A groovy invitation-only show would be lost on her.

When she said she was leaving I got up and left with her.

We sat next to each other on the L train in one of the little two-seaters. I was self-conscious being so close to her. She had a great mouth and she smelled good. Even though her shirt hid it well I'd snuck some peeks and could tell she was stacked. I wanted to see her again soon but for some reason didn't know how to tell her this.

She brought up the GBV show. Here's my window, I thought. She took out a notebook. I wrote down my e-mail address. I got off at Bedford. Hasna continued on to Grand Street. It was a pleasant night. People were out. McCarren Park looked unreal under the bright stadium lights.

Hasna arranged for me to go to the show. I met her and her friend in the East Village. She made a quick introduction and split. I watched her leave with a certain sadness. I was stuck with her friend, who as it turned out was a creep. He spoke as if he was a hugely connected and clued-in dude. He had big plans to conquer the rock world. I'd never heard of the band he was managing. They were perennial opening-act material, strictly small-time. But I drank the free cocktails and snarfed the free food. The show was a party for some technology company. Few in attendance seemed to care about Guided by Voices, who played to thirty or so people standing near the stage. Everyone else milled around chatting in the back of the room.

Erin and I crossed Graham and walked down the block. We knocked on the door at Remington's crib. Roy answered and we went through the living room to the kitchen. Sitting at the table wearing a sleeveless undershirt was Baines. He got up smiling and we hugged. I introduced him to Erin.

I hadn't seen Baines since early '97, when Paul and I stopped in Chapel Hill on the first leg of a road trip. He had some kind of office gig then. Later I heard he was writing. I heard on a lark he'd gotten a job at Burger King and written about it and the piece had been published in the *Washington Post*. Sitting at the table he told me more. An agent had seen the piece and asked to represent him. The agent asked if he wrote fiction. Baines showed him some stories and the agent was pleased. Baines applied to MFA programs and got into Columbia. He was returning to North

Carolina in a few days but would be back at the end of the summer to start classes. The only thing was his sublet wouldn't be ready yet, it was being remodeled. He was going to need a place to stay for a few weeks and said if we heard of anything to let him know.

—What about your middle room? said Erin.

—What?

—In your apartment, that middle room.

—You have an extra room? said Baines.

—Sort of.

—Well what do you think. Maybe I could sort of check it out.

I told him there were no windows. He said he didn't need them just for three or four weeks. I said I'd have to walk through his room to get to the rest of the apartment. He said how bad could it be?

—It's not that bad, said Erin.

He had a little notebook. He wrote down the address.

—How fortunate we should run into each other, he said.

Baines walked through the apartment and looked at the room. He said it'd be fine for his purposes, he'd be rocking a pretty spartan arrangement. We talked about writing and the publishing game. Baines asked where I'd been sending my stuff. I pulled out the manila folder. He sat on my bed going through my rejection slips, commenting occasionally on certain magazines, reading aloud certain handwritten remarks.

Usually I thought of the folder with a certain pride, as physical evidence of a struggle that would one day pay off. But something in me changed as I watched Baines sift through those notes.

—My agent wants to try *Esquire* with a couple of my new stories, he said.

—*Esquire*. They publish good fiction.

—They used to. Fuck, man. I don't know.

—What?

He looked at the rejection slips.

—It's just so demoralizing, he said.

At work using LexisNexis I found the Burger King piece. Baines told me the idea had been to work there a month but he'd hated his coworkers and the work was shitty and he decided one night after working back-to-back doubles that he had enough material and walked off the job after a week. In the piece various unsavory characters and appalling working conditions were described, several tragicomic anecdotes relayed, and there were a few grim stats about fast-food wages and the industry as a whole.

I squared the pages and set them on the desk. I thought back on what I knew of Baines, Remington, and Ellis. I'd met them in 1996 or so when they played in a band called the Hot Ones. My band Fletcher played some shows with them in Kalamazoo and met up with them once in Knoxville, Tennessee. There was something untouchable about them. They made me want to be like them, to the extent that after talking to them I'd adopt a slight southern drawl. I remembered they'd gone to small liberal arts schools I'd never heard of that must have cost twenty grand a year at the time. I remembered many of their stories seemed to involve foreign travel, having adventures in Rome or somewhere. Ellis, the bass player, wrote a zine chronicling his travels in which he cast himself as a kind of rogue romantic, wandering the land, meeting interesting people, taking a temp job when he needed money—which he never seemed to—or so he could write something comical about having a dumb job. Now that I thought back on it, work never seemed central to any of their concerns.

I picked up the pages and skimmed them again.

One week—barely enough time to learn your coworkers' names.

* * * *

Lois gave everyone their birthday off. This wasn't official Morgan Stanley policy, just something she did to be nice. The day I turned twenty-six I sat in a laundromat on Nassau Avenue, reading and staring into the machines as they spun.

Back at the apartment a package was waiting. I checked the return address. It was from my dad. I took it up to the kitchen and opened it. Two books were inside. One was a fat volume of poetry by Czeslaw Milosz, the other was Don DeLillo's *White Noise*. I stood holding *White Noise*, turning it over in my hands. I owned two copies already, a Penguin paperback like this one and a Viking first edition hardcover.

Don DeLillo was one of my favorite writers. I'd read all of his books, some more than once. The first one I read was *White Noise*. I read it two years ago and it blew me away. I started to ape DeLillo's style in my writing. I started to think in his sentences, his actual ones and my ripoffs. I read *Underworld* next, read it sitting in my parents' basement in the lonely and scary weeks before I moved to New York. Then I read all the others, starting at the beginning, going in order of publication. A few months earlier I'd dropped three hundred dollars on a first edition of *Americana*, his first novel.

My dad couldn't have known any of this. Contact between us had been minimal. The few times we'd talked we didn't talk about books.

That night I went with Erin and Baines and some of his North Carolina pals to a Mexican restaurant on Fourteenth Street. We ate out back on a patio. I got high on sangria but couldn't shake the weird feeling I'd had all day of time getting away from me, the reins slipping from my hands.

* * * *

The next day I called my mom to get my dad's number. I dialed it that evening. Marsha answered and said happy birthday. She went on for a few minutes about Avi, who'd turned one a few months ago.

—We'd love to see you. It's just a few hours by train and we have plenty of room.

—We'll see, I said.

—I know your father would love it if you came. And Avi, we've been telling Avi all about you. He knows he has a big brother in New York. He's eager to meet you.

She said it was great talking to me. She handed the phone to my dad. I thanked him for the books and said it was strange in a way because I was already such a big Don DeLillo fan.

—Yeah, said my dad. —I always really liked him too.

I noticed a woman in the cafeteria, a real stunner. She went from station to station assessing the selections, arms folded across her chest. When she was done she and a friend met up and discussed what looked good to them and what they might get. Then they both turned and made the circuit again. She was maybe six feet tall and had long black hair pulled back in a ponytail and dark Latin-looking skin. She was wearing a skirt and had long legs and nice thin ankles and a great purposeful walk, or that's how it seemed anyway hearing her crash down in high heels. I stood there pretending to deliberate and watched her. Eventually she picked a line. I watched her a moment longer. Then I went over to one of the sandwich-ordering kiosks. I tapped my order on the touchscreen. A little paper came out. I took the paper and stood in line. Soon one of the men called my number. I paid for the sandwich and walked into the dining area. I sat by a window and ate alone. When I was done I got up and placed my tray on the conveyor belt. I took the escalator up, took the elevator to seventy, and returned to my desk. The long afternoon passed and then the days and the weeks.

One night I was watching TV. A commercial came on. It showed some young people driving in the country at night. A sad acoustic song played. There were four of them in the car, two guys and two girls. They were the only ones on the road. The guy in the backseat looked over at the girl next to him. She in turn looked up at the full moon. Soon they pulled off. They'd arrived at a house party. The driver studied the scene with mild contempt. The house was crowded and loud and there were stumbling drunken people out front yelling *woo*. No one in the car said anything or got out. They looked around at each other somewhat sadly and then the car reversed and they drove off. They were on the empty road again under the beautiful moon. The last shot was of the girl in the backseat. She turned and looked either at the guy next to her or over her shoulder into the night, her mouth slightly open, the wind blowing her hair. The Volkswagen logo appeared on the screen. By the time this happened I was nearly in tears. I wanted to rise from the floor, climb through the TV, leave my life and everything I knew behind. I wanted to be one of those kids in that car. The girl in the backseat was so incredibly lovely. What was she looking at there at the end? It couldn't have been the geek next to her. No, her face, her eyes hinted at a deeper sort of longing. She was searching for something on the dark lanes behind them that she likely wouldn't find.

—The thing about New York, said Baines, —is say you want a little peace. So where do you go? You go into Central Park and find a bench and sit down. And you're sitting there trying to groove on some nature. And you look around and you sort of stare down at that bench and you know that a million people have sat on that very same bench before you, they've all gone there trying to achieve the same little moment of peace.

It was early September. We were on the roof. There was a pause as we drank from bottles of Bud and stared at the skyline, the sky around it bright orange, slashed with swirls and ribbons of clouds.

—You ever think about leaving? said Baines.

—New York? I don't know. Sometimes.

—Where do you think you'd go, back to Michigan?

—No. I don't think so. At least not yet.

—There's a great bit in this Larry Brown book, *On Fire*, where he talks about flying to New York to go on the *Today Show* and he's mortified by the hugeness and the inhumanity of it all.

—Larry Brown. Remington lent me one of his books. *Big Bad Love.*

—What'd you think?

—I loved it.

—Yeah he's one of my favorites. He lives down in Oxford, Mississippi. I think he's buddies with Barry Hannah down there. Man, Larry Brown's got the right idea.

—What's that?

—You just, you hang out where you're from and do your own thing and if you're good enough and you're lucky, maybe the world comes to you.

—Those are big fucking ifs.

—How long you been here? Two years?

—Just about.

—Yeah man. That's long enough.

—So where do I go if I don't go to Michigan?

—You could move down south.

—I don't know. Chapel Hill was great when I was there in February but I don't think I could handle it at the height of summer.

—Sure you could, man. You get a nice cold glass of sweet tea, sit on the porch and don't move. You don't do shit. New York in the summer is a hundred times worse.

—Michigan's nice in the summer. Lotta trees and breezes. Lakes.

—Maybe New England's the place for you. Vermont.

—Could be. I've never been.

—Or Maine. What about Maine?

—What about it?

—You ever been there?

—No.

—All right, there you go. That's the place for you. Maine. You could move to Bangor and hang out with Stephen King.

—Funny you say that. I've been on a Stephen King tear recently.

—You ever read *The Stand*?

—Yeah. When I was younger. I didn't read the uncut version.

—Oh man. It's a real masterpiece. There's something incredibly satisfying about a thousand-page book you can burn through in a week.

The sun had set. We sat finishing our beers.

—Yeah man, said Baines. —You gotta get out of New York.

He was there in the mornings when I left for work and often there in the evenings when I came home. Sometimes I'd think of him sitting home writing while I was stuck in my cubicle and I'd get down on him, wondering who was paying for everything, him or his parents or what, and I'd think again how he only worked at Burger King for a week before writing his piece. Then I'd remember he really was a good writer and I'd feel like a jerk and try to push those thoughts from my mind.

We ate meals together. We sat in my room listening to records. We'd talk about the old days, playing in punk bands. We'd talk about books and writing and girls. Living with Baines made me more productive than I'd been in months. He had a thing about word counts. I'd never given them much thought. He told me Graham Greene wrote five hundred words a day. I'd never read Graham Greene and didn't care about his work but five hundred words seemed a decent amount to shoot for so that became my goal each time I sat at the desk. On weekends we'd hole up in our rooms writing and come out later and make smoothies. Good and good for you, Baines would say as we clinked glasses. We'd exchange word counts and discuss how the work had gone. He'd tell me about his workshop and show me the stories up for critique that week. I said they seemed like something I could hang with and Baines said obviously. He told me my work was good enough and said I should apply to grad school. He said I should ditch my old desktop and look into a PowerBook, he had one and it was sweet. He said he could even send a fax with it. He said New York was overrated and full of ass-holes and no kind of place to live and encouraged me to leave town. He expressed frustration that he wasn't publishing any fiction and wondered aloud what his agent was really doing for him. I listened and didn't say at least you have an agent and you've published something in a big magazine and if you're feeling down about your writing career then I should be suicidal. He bought a box of Quaker oats and practiced making granola.

Toward the end of September Baines called me at work. His sublet still wasn't ready yet, the contractors were dragging ass. He said he might need to stay another two or three weeks but he could pay me for the whole month. At the end of October we had the same conversation and I said not to worry about it, pay me whatever.

* * * *

I was sitting on the plaza enjoying the mild afternoon. I leaned back on the bench and looked up at the towers, the clouds, the sky. Up in that sky my cubicle was waiting. It couldn't have me back yet. I needed another minute. The sound of the fountain was soothing. I could've stretched out, closed my eyes, and fallen asleep. I could've gotten up, walked away from there, and never gone back. There were other worlds, other jobs, other ways to waste my life.

What the hell is wrong with me? Why can't I do this? I'm so fucking tired and I'm only twenty-six.

I heard a voice and sat up. There was a girl on a cellphone. I'd seen her around my floor and thought maybe she worked in sales. She stood a few feet away from me and was arguing mildly with the person on the other end of the line. Now and then she'd pause and gesture. I started to really like her. I liked her voice and the things she was saying. No-bullshit things and who-the-fuck-do-you-think-you're-talking-to things and when she turned around I fell in love with her ass. It was magnificent. It was a shelf. You could've set all six volumes of Proust on it.

I had a thing for black girls but she was the kind of black girl I felt I had no chance with, like maybe she'd date a white dude but not one who quivered in the men's room stuffing paper towels under his arms.

Her hair was short and parted to the side. I liked her hair. I liked how she put her arm up with her palm open and hunched her shoulders like *I don't believe what I'm hearing right now*. I liked her skin. It was smooth and beautiful. I wanted to touch it. I stared at her ass. It was giving me strength. I was stronger now than I had been five minutes ago. I could make it through the day now, maybe even the rest of the week. I wondered who she was talking to. I wanted to know her name. I watched her and she turned and I got another view. That was all I needed. The world could burn and who fucking cared about writing. That ass was a nation I would've fought and died for.

I stood up refreshed and took the escalator to the lobby. I rode the elevators back to the seventieth floor.

Election Night. Pete's Candy Store was crowded. A TV had been set up on the bar. A celebratory vibe hung in the air. Gore had won Florida, Pennsylvania, Michigan. Baines and I traded rounds of bourbon on ice. At some point things changed. The news people recanted. Florida was moved from the Gore column back into the undecided column. The mood in the bar darkened. There were grave exchanges about the Electoral College. I tried paying attention but was too drunk now and couldn't follow it. We left Pete's and walked along Lorimer Street. We stopped at Enid's and drank some more. Remington and Roy were there. Baines ran into an old friend, a pretty girl who worked at *Vogue*. I sat with her for a while and tried making time but it was no good. The bar had cleared out and Baines and I left.

The clock radio alarm went off at 6:40. I got out of bed and left a message for Ginny saying I wouldn't be in. Two hours later Baines knocked on my door.

—What the fuck? What's happening? he said.

—I don't know. Who won?

—I don't know. I'm afraid to turn on the TV.

—All right. Hold on. We'll do it together.

We went into the living room and watched the news. Later we went into the city. The streets were quiet, the atmosphere funereal. We were hungover, hungry. We went to an Indian restaurant on First Avenue for lunch.

I walked down the hallway and into the conference room. I stepped up on the vent and peered out at Manhattan, glittering under the cold winter sky. Frank and Patrick stood in Whelan's cubicle. They had their coats on and were talking and laughing. I went over and joined them.

Whelan looked good. He and his wife had split up and he'd done a one-eighty. He'd switched from glasses to contacts, was working out, had bought a new wardrobe at Banana Republic. He was even grooving someone else, a woman in his group named Lila.

We took the elevators down and walked outside. A fleet of black towncars was idling at the curb. We got into one and the driver pulled away. We cruised up the West Side Highway. I looked out the window wondering what the night would be like.

At Chelsea Piers we got out. It was bitter cold. We went inside and bought a beer at a concession stand. Gradually the others trickled in. After everyone had arrived we walked out to the gangway and boarded the party boat. It was the latest in a series of holiday gatherings. There were also steak dinners at Del Frisco's and the Strip House, lunches at Il Giglio and Bouley Bakery, paid for by the various vendors who produced our materials.

I checked my coat and sat at one of the tables. It was open bar. Charlotte asked if I wanted a drink. Yes, I said, gin and tonic. The place filled up. There were dozens of people. I didn't recognize most of them. There were people onboard from other companies too. Charlotte brought me a drink and sat next to me. We clicked glasses and drank. Whelan and Lila were at the table. They drank their drinks and sat very close and talked only to each other.

The boat started to move.

The food was terrible, shrimp cocktail and dead cheese. I went to the bar for another drink. I finished that one and went back for a third. A sound system played party music. People started to dance. The windows had fogged. You couldn't see out.

Back by the restrooms was a set of stairs. I followed them up and out to the observation deck. I couldn't stay out long. I went back in. I ran into Charlotte on her way up the stairs.

—Come out with me, she said.

—I can't go back. I was just out there. The wind—

She grabbed my arm and pulled me back out. We were the only ones out there. The wind slashed through me. Charlotte turned to face me. I picked up a vibe.

—Let's go get another drink, I said.

—In a minute.

—It's fucking cold out here, let's go back inside.

I sipped my drink and stood by the window. I cleared a circle on the glass but couldn't see through the smear. Whelan came over. He gestured toward Lila, who was talking with some people on the other side of the room.

—Lila's great, isn't she?

—Yeah Whelan, she's all right.

—She's beautiful. I'm gonna marry her someday.

I had to laugh. As far as I knew he was technically still married.

—Well I'm glad to see you in such good spirits, old boy.

—Thank you, my man.

The cocktails weren't strong but I was feeling quite high. I got misty for the past.

On this night nine years ago my high school band Brainstorm played a show in our drummer's basement. I was so in love with Daisy but knew she was at the Portage Northern Christmas dance with motherfucking Jean Pierre. At the show I screamed a loud prayer for a power failure at the dance. I made everyone shut up and pray with me.

—Let's go back to the deck, see what we're missing, said Charlotte.

—All right.

We walked through the crowd, up the stairs, and outside. We were by the World Trade Center. The towers filled the black sky, glittering and magical and cold.

Charlotte skipped forward a few steps, turned around, and smiled.

—Don't you just feel like you own this city?

—No.

She came over and stood close to me.

—You know what it's like when you want something so bad and you're just about to get it? she said.

She put her arms around me and kissed me. I tried kissing back for a moment but the styles were bad. I pulled away. I went back inside and watched the party unfold as if in a dream.

Frank sat glumly at a table nursing a cup of coffee. Patrick walked toward us holding a beer. Nancy drunkenly yelled at Ginny's boyfriend Ward, pulling his arm practically out of its socket, telling him he needed to get his woman out on that dance floor and dance with her *now*. Nancy's husband Avery threw his arms up and screamed. He turned to the window and wrote *Avery N Nance* in the fog. I looked for Whelan and Lila but they'd disappeared. I walked upstairs and went out on the deck. The boat was under the Statue of Liberty. I'd never seen it this close before. Its ghostly blue form hovered against the cold sky. It looked like a giant unfeeling monster with blank eyes. I leaned over the railing looking down at the water. I went back inside.

I was sitting alone sipping another drink. Charlotte staggered through the crowd and leaned down over me.

—What are you doing later?

—Nothing. Taking a car service home.

—You could come to my place.

Patrick stood behind her. He shook his head and smiled.

—I can't tonight, I said.

—Come on. Don't you want it? It'd be so amazing.

—I'm sure it would be.

—Come on. Don't you wanna jerk off in my mouth?

She opened her mouth and jabbed a finger in and out of it.

Patrick said her name and put a hand on her arm. She turned and fell forward and snapped at him, saying he was too fucking blond. They drifted away from me. Everything blurred. The boat was out on the dark water a long time.

Baines moved out a week later. He left me a bottle of Maker's Mark with a shot glass upside down over the neck. A week after that I got a letter from *Glimmer Train* saying I was a finalist in their Short Story Award for New Writers competition. The story wasn't published and the only recognition I received was my name on a list with twenty-two other finalists. But it gave me the hit of confidence I needed and allowed me to think I'd gotten better as a writer and that publishing something was an imminent reality. I took the story to work and made multiple copies. I stuffed them in large Morgan Stanley envelopes, addressed to the ten or so best magazines I could think of. I brought the stack to the mail bins in the One World Trade lobby, kissed each envelope for luck before dropping it in.

I spent a week in Michigan for Christmas. I was supposed to return New Year's Eve but a snowstorm rolled in and my flight was canceled. My parents and I drove home from the Grand Rapids airport in silence. Ed took the curving rural back roads. We passed through frozen white landscapes and arrived home after dark. I had a great feeling walking into the warm house with my bag, as if we'd gone back in time and I'd only just now arrived. We watched Times Square on TV and drank a toast at midnight. I flew back to New York on the first day of 2001.

Is This a New Fear?

I stood on the concourse behind the PATH train escalators wearing headphones, watching as endless streams of humans were delivered into the mouth of the mall. I walked through the lobby and got in an elevator. I stopped at the cafeteria and bought a medium Starbucks, an everything bagel, and a bottle of Poland Spring water. In my cubicle I opened the cupboard, took down a jar of Skippy, spread peanut butter on the bagel, read the *Daily News*, and ate.

In the men's room I sat on the high toilet in the last stall, awaiting release. For a moment the only sounds were the soothing rush of water in pipes and the occasional creak of the tower as it moved imperceptibly in the wind. Then I heard toilet paper being quickly unrolled, followed every few seconds by a flush. The noise was coming from two stalls away. It went on for several minutes. There was a violence to the action, as if the man doing it was in a hurry or upset. I stood and tucked my shirt in and exited the stall, slamming the door a little to see what would happen. Nothing did. I paused briefly after washing my hands to see if the person would cease these wild actions. He didn't. He kept unrolling the toilet paper and flushing the toilet, unrolling and flushing, unrolling and flushing. I waited another few seconds and then left.

I walked through legal and circled around. I walked through sales and then back to marketing. Nancy stopped me and told me the new *Sports Illustrated* had arrived. I thanked her and took the magazine to my desk. I read it a while and then set it aside. I turned in my chair and unlocked my computer. I opened the document I'd been working on and highlighted a random block of text. I spread some papers around on the desk. I picked up the phone and dialed Samantha's home number. The answering machine clicked on and I punched in her code. I listened again to the message. It was from a guy named Rene who had an accent of some kind. He addressed her as Sam and referred to his cell-phone as the mo-*bile*. I hung up and sat there. All the little sounds in the office were amplified a thousandfold. Whelan walked by and saw me.

—Oh yes, he said.

The bar was on Avenue B just south of Fourteenth Street and had a special on Thursdays, three-dollar pints of Guinness. Baines was sitting at the bar talking on his cellphone when I arrived. I sat next to him and ordered a pint. The local news was playing with the sound down on the TV overhead. Baines finished the conversation and set down his phone.

—Sorry about that, he said.

—That's okay. How's the new crib?

—It's an easier commute, I'll tell you that.

I laughed. —Yeah I guess Greenpoint's pretty far from Columbia.

—What about you? How's the writing going?

—Good. You know I got my holiday bonus and took the plunge. I bought a PowerBook.

—How do you like it?

—I have to say it's pretty nice.

I told him about the *Glimmer Train* contest and a new story I'd started about going to my dad's girlfriend's apartment for breakfast shortly after I moved to the city. He told me he'd finished a draft of a story about Vikings.

—Vikings?

—Yeah.

—I'd love to read it.

—We should meet up and do a swap one of these nights. Maybe next week.

—I'm open, I said.

—You given any more thought to grad school?

—I gave it all kinds of thought. But I blew the deadlines for Columbia and NYU.

—Ah shit.

—I know. I fucked up. I'll have to wait till next year.

—Maybe not. What about Brooklyn College? You looked at them yet?

—Brooklyn College? No.

—They have a later deadline, I think. Apparently they're shoring things up over there. Michael Cunningham's taking over the MFA program.

—Michael Cunningham? Really?

—Columbia wanted him. I'm not sure what happened. Anyway. Brooklyn College. Look into it.

—I will.

We drank three pints each and left the bar. I saw double as we walked toward Fourteenth Street, everything swam.

On the corner of Avenue A and Fourteenth I looked over at Stuyvesant Town. A thought sparked in the murk. I told Baines I was going to shove off here and go see a friend. I crossed the street and walked into the vast complex of hulking shadowy buildings. I'd helped Eve move in here. When was that? Long time ago. I hadn't seen her since the night she and Samantha and I all went to the sushi place to celebrate our mutual first days of work. I walked to One Stuyvesant Oval and entered the vestibule. I squinted at the list of residents' names. She was sub-letting illegally and it took me a moment to remember the name. Glass. I picked up the phone and dialed the number.

Eve please answer, please buzz me in, I need this so badly I need to see you so badly now please Eve let me come up I only want to sit on your sofa and close my eyes and lay back and have the world stop for a few minutes and have my life stop and have you there next to me Eve oh my god please.

No one answered. I tried again. I put the phone in the cradle and walked out into the cold.

Sylvia's Beaker laugh and her heavy footfalls like elephant stomps through the office. Her little fat hands wiggling, the fingers opening and contracting with every step. Max's ceaseless banter and his stale jokes and the life-size cutout of Austin Powers in his office grinning his huge grin, pointing both fingers, a motion sensor device and a little speaker in back and all day long Austin Powers goes *Yeah baby. Yeah baby. Very shagadelic. Yeah baby. Very shagadelic. Yeah baby. Yeah baby. Yeah baby.* I waited till he was gone, walked into his office, and switched the thing off. He came back and noticed it wasn't talking and turned it on again. Lois calling meetings to talk about branding, rebranding, outside-the-box thinking, wordmarks, realignments, fresh ideas, new directions, the Internet, the Intranet, content-repurposing, the imminent 360 peer-review system. Passing out Xeroxed copies of *Who Moved My Cheese?* Max responding days later with his own thick packet of photocopied articles from business magazines talking about change, paradigm shifts, adaptation, get-ting from here to there. Shirley selling spiral-bound cookbooks made by children with learning disabilities for some vague char-ity. She came to my desk and stood over me, her neck splattered with red birthmarks, the flesh of her arms thick, dimpled, hanging. I wanted to say no, scream in her face, tell her to go fuck herself. Instead I told her I'd think about it. She came back later. I bought a cookbook.

I took the elevators down and wandered the concourse. I scoped the sale rack at Banana Republic. I went to Borders and stood at the new-release table dreaming of the day I might see my own book there but left feeling certain that day would never arrive. I walked through the lobby, took the elevators up, walked to my cubicle, sat. At some point the phone rang. It was Samantha.

—What are you, typing?

—Just a quick thing. I'm done now.

—Don't call me and type.

—Sorry. I'm working, she said.

—Well don't call me and work.

—Have you been listening to my messages?

—What?

—Have you been calling my machine?

—No I haven't.

—It's okay if you have, I'm not mad.

—Well. Fine. But I haven't.

—Are you sure?

—Yes.

—All right. I believe you. How's work?

—Fine.

—That's it, just fine?

—Yeah.

—We should get together sometime.

—Is that a joke?

—No. Why don't we get together for a drink.

—A drink? Are you crazy?

—No. Why?

—I don't think so.

—Come on, one drink. It'll be good. We could talk.

—Talk. You wanna talk?

—Yeah.

—Talk to Rene. Give him a call on the mo-*bile.*

She started to say something. I slammed down the phone.

But I went to meet her anyway on a cold and rainy Friday night. We met at Whiskey Blue in the W Hotel. All the men wore suits or sport coats and had gelled hair and smiled hugely and had loud confident laughs. The women were pretty and sleek and sipped colorful cocktails. Samantha ordered a martini. I ordered a Maker's Mark and ginger ale. I hadn't seen her in eight months and I was nervous. We exchanged tense pleasantries. We ordered more drinks. I asked about our breakup. She revealed nothing new. She'd been confused, she didn't know how to handle it, it was a mistake, she knew, doing it over the phone. But she'd been upset and scared of confrontation and had done the best she could under the circumstances. I kept laughing as she talked. At one point she stopped. I thought I saw tears in her eyes. She turned away and when she looked back they were gone.

We walked across the hall to another bar. We drank some more. She touched my arm and we held hands. Outside in a freezing rain we waited several minutes for a cab. One pulled over and we headed uptown. I moved next to her on the seat and we kissed. I moved my hand up her thigh, up the front of her shirt. I unbuttoned her shirt, slid my hand inside, pulled down her bra.

In the deli next to her building she bought a six pack. We went upstairs. Her apartment looked and smelled the same. We sat on the couch drinking the beer, listening to the Weezer CD I'd bought her all those months ago. In her bedroom I reached over and looked in the drawer for a condom but found only an empty wrapper. I went in anyway and she said be careful, don't come inside me. I said you used the last condom with him didn't you? She didn't answer. I said you had unprotected sex with him didn't you? Then I shut up and it went on for a while and then it ended.

For the rest of the night I drifted in and out of a vague sleep. Early in the morning with gray light at the window we did it again. I got out of bed and as I was dressing noticed one of my shirts on the floor of her closet. She walked me to the door wearing only a T-shirt.

—Do you wanna get some coffee? she said.

—No.

—Are you sure?

—Yeah. I'm gonna . . . I have to get going.

—Okay.

It was still raining. I took the 4 downtown and caught the L. I walked home from Bedford Avenue in the rain.

After I showered I sat on the couch drinking coffee and thinking about the night before. It was a dull gray day. I was confused and depressed. I turned on the TV. Every channel showed the inauguration. George W. Bush stood with his hand on the bible. He took the oath of office and made a speech.

Two weeks later on another cold wet night I walked with Erin past Samantha's building. It felt like returning to the scene of a crime. I stared straight ahead as we passed. Wet snow flew at my eyes.

We took our seats in the auditorium of the 92nd Street Y. Chang Rae Lee read first. I didn't know his work and hardly heard a word he said. When he was finished Jonathan Franzen, another writer I'd never heard of, came out and introduced Don DeLillo. The introduction was pretentious and rambling and mentioned the sometimes regrettable things writers say on Charlie Rose, the implication being that DeLillo wasn't guilty of these missteps because he existed at a remove from the scene.

DeLillo was shorter and thinner than I'd imagined. He wore a green work shirt, jeans, winter boots, and thick black glasses. He read from *The Body Artist*, his new book. During the reading I heard Erin sniffling. There were tears on her face. Out on the street I turned to her as we walked through the snow.

—Hey were you crying in there?

—I was. Something came over me as he was reading and I lost it.

—In a good way?

—Yeah. In a good way. It was beautiful.

I was standing at the sink with my mouth open, investigating the crevices of my throat in the mirror. There was a little white spot on my tonsil that had me alarmed. I hadn't realized there was anyone else in the men's room. Then I heard movement, the rapid unrolling of toilet paper, and every few seconds a flush.

Him again.

I washed my hands for a second time and remained where I was. I stood quite still in the hope that he would forget I was there and eventually come out. But two or three minutes passed and he didn't stop. Quietly I grabbed a paper towel and pretended to dry my hands so that if someone came in I would look more natural. Sure enough, Patterson from sales walked in. The noises stopped. I threw away the paper towel and left.

So it wasn't Patterson.

And it wasn't Whelan, who was on the phone when I got back to my desk. After he hung up I went over and told him what had happened in the men's room. I said it was the second time I'd heard it and asked if he'd heard it before. He said no. I returned to my desk but couldn't concentrate. I went back to the men's room. There was no one in the stalls. I opened the door to the first one and it was normal. I opened the next one and stepped back in mild shock. Toilet paper filled the bowl. It was piled to the seat and spilled out in long unbroken strands over the sides. It was draped around the handle and covered the floor. The roll had been emptied, used down to the cardboard, and there was toilet paper dust and little bits on the tiles.

—Jesus Christ, I said aloud.

I called in sick and went into the city. I walked through the East Village, down to Canal Street, and then back up into Washington Square Park. The park was relatively empty. I sat on a bench looking at the World Trade Center. Everywhere I turned I could see the towers. The sight of them filled me with a vague sense of guilt. I walked to Carmine Street and met Baines at his pad. We went to the Waverly diner for lunch. After that I walked up Sixth Avenue to Twentieth Street, stopped at Lava, and saw Erin. She was sitting alone in the big empty room, watching an old black-and-white TV she'd plugged in with a long extension cord. We rapped for a while. I flipped through the *Post*. I got up and left. I wandered over to Seventh Avenue and caught an uptown train. I walked along 125th Street for a while then circled around, went south several blocks, and got back on the train. Back in Brooklyn a rejection note was waiting, one of several I'd received that week. It was a form note with no handwriting and I wasn't sure what story it was for. I put it in the folder with the others. There was a stack of pages on my desk. I took them into the living room with a pen and began reading. It was a draft of the story I'd written about my dad and Marsha. I'd called it "Blueberry Pancakes." I had a good feeling about this one, someone would go for it, for sure. When I was done with the edit I returned the pages to my desk to deal with later when I had more energy.

* * * *

The doctor looked at the scale and wrote down my weight. She put the sleeve on my arm, squeezed the bulb, and wrote down my blood pressure. She moved a stethoscope around on my chest and back and told me to take big breaths. She tied my arm with a rubber tube and drew vials of blood. She pressed around on my stomach. She lifted my underwear and felt my balls. She left the room and I dressed and walked into her office. She asked if there was anything else I'd like to discuss.

—There is one thing, I said.

—Yes?

—I have this . . . I'm very . . . I seem to have a deep fear of flying.

—Seem to?

—No I do. Flying is very hard for me.

—Is this a new fear?

—No. I've had it a while now. Years.

—How bad is it, would you say?

—Every time I set foot on an airplane I think I'm going to die.

—I see. Are there any physical symptoms?

I told her there were and went through the list.

—How often do you fly?

—Not very often. As infrequently as possible. But I'm doing it next week.

She asked a few more questions. I answered them truthfully. She listened and nodded. She reached for her pad.

—I'm writing you a prescription for Xanax. I'm starting you at a low dose and I'm only giving you ten pills. You'll take one or two a little before your flight—say an hour or so—and we'll see how it goes.

Before leaving for the airport I took one of the pills. I felt nothing. After checking in and going through security I stopped at a drinking fountain and swallowed another one. Half an hour later I still felt nothing. I took two more. At last a dim warm feeling began its slow crawl through me. It didn't go deep enough. Nothing could stem the terror.

The earth fell away. The plane banked hard. I was sweating and terrified all the way to Grand Rapids.

I drove into Kalamazoo and met up with Greg, who was visiting from Chicago. He asked how things were in New York. Not great, I said. I told him it was next to impossible to get any writing done and my job had me on the edge of a nervous fucking breakdown. What a coincidence, he said, I'm in the same boat.

Greg wrote marketing copy for a greeting card company. He said the people there wanted blood. He said he'd tried to be nice to them at first but they could tell it wasn't his true personality and that made them hate him more, they all wanted to kill him, they'd wanted to kill him the moment they set eyes on him. Work was so traumatic that all he could do at the end of the day was sit stunned playing video games. He hadn't written any poems in a long time.

After a while I left and walked to Club Soda. I hadn't been there in years. I got a beer and stood by the stage. The guys in Rollinghead came out and began their set. They'd reunited recently and this was their first show in years. As I watched them I thought of all the shows in the past, here and at Harvey's and elsewhere in Kalamazoo, Rollinghead shows and other shows, all the shows I'd played in bands I was in, all the shows of my friends' bands and touring bands, playing in basements for two or three or five dollars. I drank my beer and mouthed the words to the songs.

I noticed a girl staring at me. I thought I recognized her but wasn't sure. Then she walked over and I saw it was one of my former students from Portage Northern. Family sociology. Fourth hour. Donna Gibbs. I did some quick math. Either she was newly twenty-one or here with a fake ID.

—Mr. Charles.

—Hello Donna.

—What are you doing here?

—Watching the band. What are you doing here?

—I'm here with my boyfriend.

As she said this her boyfriend walked over, put his arm around her, and gave me a hard stare. She introduced me as Mr. Charles. He kept looking at me.

—I'm gonna go get some money, baby, he said.

—All right.

I'd always thought Donna was foxy. She looked foxy now. She was maybe six years younger than me. Six years had seemed like a lot when I was teaching. It didn't seem like much now. She asked what I'd been up to. I said I lived in New York. She said she went to Michigan State now and was only in town for the weekend.

—Mr. Charles if I ask you something do you promise to tell me the truth?

—Sure.

—Why did you write me that letter?

—Letter?

I honestly had no idea what she was talking about.

—I don't know, Donna. I don't remember writing you any letter.

—Yeah well. You did.

—No I don't doubt it, it's just . . . what did the letter say?

—What did it say?

—Was it serious or funny?

She thought for a second and then spoke but the music was loud and I couldn't hear her. I thought she said funny. I looked in her eyes. Donna returned my stare.

* * * *

The next night a friend called and asked me to go out but I decided to stay in. I went into the living room, grabbed a pillow, and plopped down on the floor. My mom was flicking through the channels. She stopped on *Citizen Kane*. Kane whispered *Rosebud*, the snow globe broke open. Ten minutes in I heard snoring—Ed asleep in his huge recliner. My mom and I watched the movie as Ed snored away. After they'd gone to bed I sat at the dining room table in silence. Once in a while a car passed by on G Avenue. Hide this in your heart. Carry it with you to New York.

Sometime before nine I was reading the *Daily News*. I heard Whelan come in. He passed by my cubicle, stopped, came back.

—Oh no, he said.

I looked up. His jacket was open. We were wearing the same sweater. Not similar—identical. A green collared sweater from Banana Republic.

—Something like this was bound to happen, I said. —Between you and me, Patrick and Frank. I'm just surprised it didn't happen sooner.

He laughed. —This'll be a fun day.

—No.

—No?

I pushed my chair back and stood.

—I'm gonna go down and get another shirt.

—What? Don't be ridiculous.

—Whelan I'm already ridiculous. *This* is ridiculous. But I'm not gonna sit here all day and have people come by and make their stupid fucking comments. It's bad enough when two people just wear something similar. Oh I didn't get the memo, I didn't know it was blue shirt day, ha ha. Over and over, all day long. Imagine when they see this.

—It'll be annoying.

—Annoying? I'd rather take poison, I said.

—You feel strongly about it.

—One of us has to take the hit here and I'm willing to step up. Even though, as we know, I owned the shirt first.

—So you're saying I should be the one to go buy a new shirt.

—No. I got this one. But if it happens again . . .

—If it happens again I'll take the hit.

The beautiful woman I'd first seen in the cafeteria—tall with dark hair and dark skin—was now on my radar nonstop. I'd started seeing her regularly in the cafeteria and in the lobby in the morning or at night walking out. I'd started timing my comings and goings roughly according to what I could glean of her schedule. I'd learned things about her hearing her talk in the elevator.

Her name was Jasmine. She was a broker's assistant on the seventy-third floor. Her birthday was in May. She was three years younger than me. She lived on Staten Island. She loved Frappucinos. She used Pantene shampoo.

I would stand next to her wanting like crazy to talk to her but there was never an opening, never a way of doing it without seeming like a creep. My crush ballooned into an obsession. Everyone knew about it. I bent Whelan's ear daily, told him I'd fallen in love with her, that I wanted to move to Staten Island to be with her. We'd watch TV in the evenings, have Friday night dinners at the Olive Garden after hitting the mall. It would be a different, better kind of life.

My coworkers knew Jasmine by sight. They called her the Girl from the Seventy-third Floor. They'd tell me when they spotted her, as if they'd seen a celebrity.

We made eye contact one day as I was getting off the elevator. I took it as a sign that this was the day to reach out to her. At lunch I walked to the South Street Seaport and sat on a bench staring at the Brooklyn Bridge for inspiration. I returned to my desk, opened Outlook, located Jasmine in the directory, and clicked her name into the box.

I discarded the message without writing a word. I took the pill bottle from the desk and popped a Xanax. My doctor had given me a new prescription—a higher dosage, a full bottle this time.

Because nothing changes. The long afternoons kill you, the endless hours between two and five. You never thought three hours could last that long but they do. You never realized you could get so exhausted from just sitting but you do.

The concourse saves you.

The men's room saves you.

The women save you.

You fantasize about fucking virtually every woman you see.

Billie and Sarah work in sales. They're good friends. Billie's a temp, thin and pretty with braces on her teeth. Her braces make her that much cuter, you think. Sarah's permanent. She's someone's assistant. You met Billie first, saw her on the escalator at Borders. She was going down, you were coming up. You recognized her. You locked eyes and she smiled. I know you, she said. You went to find her later. She was sitting with Sarah. This made you happy—it was Sarah's ass that had been the source of such rejuvenation on the plaza that day. You became fast friends. Now you visit them often, lingering at their desks for ten, fifteen minutes or more.

Don't you have work to do? they ask.

Not really, you say.

The work you have, in your busiest week, takes three hours maximum. You update brochures. Once in a while you write one. You assemble a quarterly newsletter for FAs called *Fund Update Quarterly*. There's a masthead on back, your name in a box next to the words MANAGING EDITOR. You fought for this. It seemed important to you.

The print runs for this newsletter and the brochures are many thousands of copies. Meanwhile you can't get a story published. You can't get a poem published. You can't get an essay published. You can't get a short play published. You haven't tried but you're pretty sure you couldn't get a motherfucking haiku published.

Is your work that much worse than what appears in the lit mags? You think not but then again who knows? Writing is a confidence game. Often you lack confidence. Maybe your work is in fact worse and that's why it keeps coming back to you, week after week, a steady stream of envelopes containing your manuscripts, little form notes clipped to the first page.

Dear Writer,

Thank you for giving us the opportunity to consider your work. Unfortunately . . .

When you were younger and dreaming of being a writer you never thought of how you'd make a living while waiting to get published. There'd been no mention of it in college and you were so naive and so arrogant it never crossed your mind.

College was a hundred years ago. College was a kid's dream. *This*—this is reality. These endless dull days. These lonely nights. The dull comforts of money.

The other day you went to the Citibank ATM in the One World Trade lobby, took out a hundred dollars, and saw to your astonishment that you had over five thousand dollars left, with rent for the month already paid. You've never had anywhere near that much money. It gave you a warm feeling as you walked through the lobby with your cash in your pocket, took the elevators up and returned to your cubicle.

Maybe it's not so bad after all. Maybe I can make it work. Someone will publish me someday. I can still write on weekends—

The feeling fades quickly.

Boredom returns.

Boredom breeds despair.

You walk through legal and sales. You hear voices, ringing phones, little computer blips announcing the arrival of new e-mail. You go into the conference room, step up on the vent, put your face to the glass. You think of jumping and how it would feel that first second in the air. Would you go into shock or die of a heart attack before you even hit the ground? Or maybe those are just myths.

Only one way to find out.

You return to your desk. Your phone console tells you it's 2:35.

How could it only be 2:35? You thought it was at least four. Your thoughts race and crash, scream and burn. You are nothing. You're dying. You're already dead.

Borders saves you.

Mrs. Field's saves you.

Banana Republic saves you.

The Starbucks counter in the cafeteria saves you.

The Internet saves you.

The Internet depletes you.

The women save you.

Jasmine saves you.

The elevator doors part and there she is, she and a friend in mid-conversation. You step in and the doors close. The car begins its descent.

—What's that one book? says Jasmine. —The one where it's like two guys in Depression times and one of them is retarded? And the retarded guy is like obsessed with bunny rabbits.

The friend hesitates. —Of Mice and Men?

—Yeah. That's it. Of Mice and Men. That was like the only book I read in high school. It was kinda funny though. I liked it. What were those two guys' names, the main guys? Lenny and— who was the other guy?

—Squiggy, says her friend and they laugh. —No I don't know. I forget.

George! your mind screams. Say it! George!

—Lenny and shit—what was it? says Jasmine.

Fucking George! Just say it! It's so easy! Say George!

—Anyway that's who Hollis and Peterson remind me of, Lenny and that other guy. The brains and retard.

Again they laugh.

—You're right, says her friend.

On forty-four you get out and catch the next elevator. You stand behind her and stare, close enough to smell the Pantene.

I want to kiss you. His name is George.

Finally, in the throes of a chest-clutching panic, I wrote her: *This is embarrassing but I've been seeing you around and wanted to introduce myself. No pressure to write back or anything, I just wanted to say hi.* Jasmine wrote back: *Don't be embarrassed, you should have said hi to me, I don't bite :).*

I was stunned.

I did a tour of the office and returned to my desk.

We exchanged a few e-mails. My pit sweat cascaded. I took a Xanax. Whelan, I said, you won't fucking believe what's happening, I'm communicating with Jasmine. He didn't believe me. I told him to come over.

—Unreal, he said when he looked at my screen. —You finally did it.

—You didn't think I would?

—Frankly no, he said.

At 10:30 I had to go to a meeting. It took an enormous effort to sit composed at the shiny table. It felt like I was having a heart attack.

Jasmine and I exchanged another round of messages. I vaguely floated the notion of a meeting, said maybe I'd run into her in the elevator sometime. She wrote back saying if I wanted to I could meet her and her friends someday for drinks after work. Whelan! I nearly shouted, Whelan listen to this! I wrote back asking for her extension. She didn't respond. That's okay, I thought, she's busy, she'll get back to me soon. By the end of the day I still hadn't heard from her. She didn't write back the next day either. I sent her another message, three lines it took twenty minutes to write. She didn't respond. I went into a freefall, filled pages of a Morgan Stanley legal pad riffing on how pathetic and miserable I was.

I dreamed of Jasmine. I was on a bed facedown. She was lying on top of me. Hey lonesome, she said right before we kissed.

In real life I hid the next time I saw her. She was by the escalator on forty-four. I ducked into an elevator bank, went back up to seventy.

One evening a letter from Brooklyn College was waiting. I stood in the vestibule turning it over in my hands. I opened it and read the first few lines. It told me I'd been accepted into their MFA program for fiction writing. For the first time in a century someone had said yes.

In the lobby of the Sheraton on Seventh Avenue I sat in a chair looking out at the street. Soon a cab pulled up and Ed got out and then my mom. The cabbie opened the trunk and removed their bags. They entered the lobby and checked into the hotel. I helped them bring their stuff to their room. Then we walked down Seventh Avenue to Times Square. Ed had never been to New York and looked around in amazement.

—Christ the whole city ain't like this, is it?

I laughed. —No. Don't worry.

—I ain't complainin. It's kinda neat.

* * * *

The next day was Friday, cooler and overcast. I'd taken the day off and woke up early and met them at their hotel. We went to Battery Park and waited in the long line for the ferries to Ellis Island and the Statue of Liberty.

On Ellis Island, almost by accident, I found Ed's grandmother's name on one of the plaques. My mom took pictures of Ed down on one knee staring at it. On the boat going back she took pictures of the trade center, the towers disappearing into the mist and low clouds.

—You won't be able to see much, I said.

—Maybe it'll clear up a little.

At the security desk they were photographed and given temporary ID cards. We went up to seventy and I showed them my cubicle. People came over to meet them—Ginny, Frank, Patrick, Whelan. We went into the conference room but all you could see through the windows was gray. My mom told Ed the view really was spectacular and they should really come back sometime when the day was clear. We walked down the hall and they met some more people and then we left.

At dinner they talked about how nice the office was and what nice people I worked with. Ed in particular was impressed.

—Boy you got it made there.

—Yeah? How so?

—Goddamn. You just sit at a desk. Talk to people all day.

—Honey he has to do more than that.

—Sometimes not much more, I said.

—That's all right, said Ed. —Beats workin in a paper mill.

—I guess so.

—You guess so? Shit.

—Ed liked seeing all the cute girls.

—Oh yeah?

—The women didn't look like that at the mill, that's for sure.

I laughed. —No they didn't.

—He liked that one girl we met, what was her name?

—I don't know.

—She had sort of dirty blonde hair? Real cute?

—I don't know.

—The one that we met by the doors as we were leaving?

—Jenny?

—Jenny. That's right.

—You like Jenny? I said.

—She was real pretty. Seemed real nice.

—Jenny's all right. I don't know her really.

—Well if I was you I'd get on the stick. Get to know her really.

—She has a boyfriend.

—That's all right. She ain't married, is she?

—No.

—Okay. There you go.

My mom laughed. —You sound like Art.

—Christ. Don't say that.

—No but we enjoyed meeting everyone. They all seemed nice.

—They are. They're nice. I work with good people mostly.

—And they're payin you how much? said Ed. —Fifty thousand?

—It's fifty-four now. I got a raise.

—Fifty-four thousand? Shit. I'd shovel out a room full of chest-high shit upside-down for fifty-four thousand. Boy you don't know how good you got it up there.

Several people were in the copy room reminiscing gaily about the bombing. I made copies and listened to them talking and laughing. Then the stories dried up and the group dispersed. I stopped at Dana's cubicle on the way back to my desk.

—Dana do you realize where we are right now?

—Work?

—Beyond that.

—Where?

—We're at ground fucking zero for a major terrorist attack.

—Bryan. God forbid, she said smiling.

—Dana it's true, said Whelan from the other side of the cubicle wall. —We need to establish a contingency plan.

—That's right. Schedule a meeting. Get Lois in there. Ginny. John Long. Everyone. We need to talk about what we're gonna do when the shit goes down.

—Sure, she said. —I'll set up a time.

—Dana you're laughing, said Whelan.

—Yes why are you laughing? This is a serious matter.

—Okay.

—I don't think she believes you, said Whelan.

—Do you believe me, Dana?

She sat there smiling. —God forbid.

—Dana you have the most beautiful eyes. Have I ever told you that?

—Bryan. You're bad.

—I think I'm falling in love with you, I said.

Number Six

Now it was summer. Things began to unravel. I saw Erin some-times but spent more time alone. I went to work and came home and tried to write. Sometimes I was able to, more often I wasn't. I started to think about quitting my job. I thought about school in the fall and writing new material for my workshops. I could use old stories but I wanted to write new ones. I knew I wouldn't be able to do sustained good work as long as I sat in an office forty hours a week. Maybe some people could do it writing only in the mornings or the evenings or on weekends but I couldn't make it work. I'd tried every combination of writing with a day job but I was always tired and never got enough done. And the work I did pro-duce suffered from lack of focus and my constant fatigue. I learned that when I wasn't writing I was incredibly unhappy and hated myself. And I wasn't writing most of the time now.

I hated my job, it meant nothing to me, but I was scared to quit. The work was easy and I was making good money and had good health insurance. These were things I couldn't see living without, at least not in New York. For a while I thought I might get laid off. The markets were in turmoil. The Morgan Stanley stock price was falling. A nervous feeling crept into the office and lingered. Lois called a meeting and said cutbacks and layoffs were inevitable but told us not to worry, no one was being let go yet.

Keep your heads down and keep working and you'll be all right, she said, pantomiming fingers on a keyboard. The people in this room are the future of the firm, she said. Then she rescinded her unofficial birthday-off policy.

When the layoffs came they affected only two administrative assistants in sales and I was relieved.

Meanwhile the toilet paper guy haunted me. I continued to find evidence of his mania. Toilets choked with paper. Paper strewn on the floor. Once when he was in there I peeked under the stall and saw that he was facing forward, which meant he *stood* shoving toilet paper in the toilet and flushing it for minutes at a time. I tried to figure out who it was from his pant cuffs and shoes but it was standard issue business-casual gear and could have belonged to anyone. I questioned others in the office. Patrick and Frank had both heard him. They found it mildly amusing, vaguely perplexing, nothing more.

Who was this madman? I had to know.

I spent more and more time away from my desk. I walked to the Strand and looked through the stacks. I walked to the Seaport and stared at the water. I sat on a bench in the graveyard behind St. Paul's Chapel and read.

You must change your life.

I don't know how.

But I was seeing Paul and Trish more and that was a good thing. They'd lived briefly in Jersey City but their roommate had fucked them over and in the spring they'd moved farther out to a town called Fair Lawn. Paul and Trish had always been good to me. I'd known them so long and I was losing track of who I was and they helped me remember.

One Saturday I went to see them. I took the PATH to Hoboken and boarded a Bergen County Line train. The train left the station and rolled along through New Jersey. I stared out the window thinking of nothing. Then I saw myself on a night a long time ago, when I was sixteen. I was at a house on West Main Street in Kalamazoo, across from a strip mall. I was in a strange girl's room in a beanbag chair on the floor. The girl was on top of me and we were kissing. I was friends with the girl's roommate but didn't know this girl. She was four years older than me, had grown up in Muskegon, and had a brother. Those were the only things I knew. She smelled like patchouli. She pulled off my pants. She went to lower herself onto me and I felt vague genital contact and then came everywhere and the whole thing was done. I lay terrified in the beanbag not knowing what had happened. To this day I'm not sure. The girl curled into my arm. I stared at the ceiling in the darkness wondering what I'd just done. A couple weeks later she called and said she had chlamydia and there was a strong chance that I had it too.

This is a story, I thought, I'm going to write this.

I closed my eyes trying to keep everything together, writing random sentences in my head.

I met my dad and Marsha at the Bryant Park Cafe. They smiled when they saw me. I smiled back. Sitting in a stroller in front of them was Avi. I'd expected to feel strange or sad seeing Avi. But he was just a two-year-old in a stroller and I didn't feel much. Maybe if he'd looked more like me . . . but he was small and thin and had reddish hair. He looked more like Marsha, with maybe a bit of my dad's mouth. I've always more resembled my mom's side of the family but I have green eyes like my dad.

They were on their way back to DC from Rhode Island, where Marsha's family lived. As we ate I kept looking at Avi. Now I was beginning to feel strange. He squirmed in his stroller and started to cry. He cried loudly and I looked around at the other tables in embarrassment. Marsha said he was tired.

They asked what was new. I told them I was going to grad school in the fall and mentioned some other things. Avi kept squirming and crying. His cries were loud and shrill and I couldn't think. Finally Marsha went away with him. My dad and I sat there. He looked at me, smiling proudly.

—You know Avi's a cute kid but you were really pretty cute too.

Afterward they asked—nearly begged—me to visit, told me again and again they had plenty of room. They said Avi really was looking forward to getting to know me. I smiled and looked at Avi.

—Is that right? I asked him.

Avi stared up at me, half asleep.

—Oh yeah, said Marsha, —we have your picture up and he looks at it and he just, he talks about you all the time. Don't you, Avi? Avi? He's shy right now but trust me.

—All right, I said, —we'll see.

I said goodbye to them and walked out of the park. I didn't feel like getting on the subway so I headed south with no destination in mind. I walked down through Union Square and took a left on Fourteenth Street. At Avenue A I turned into Stuyvesant Town. I went into Eve's lobby and rang her buzzer.

—Hello?

—It's Bryan Charles.

—*Bryan Charles?*

—Yeah. What are you doing?

—Nothing. Andrea's here.

—Can I come up?

She paused for a second.

—Why don't I come down.

—All right.

She came out of the elevator into the vestibule. We went outside and sat on a bench facing a playground. We sat for a moment watching kids play.

—How've you been? she asked.

—All right. How have you been?

—Good. So. What have you been up to?

—Not much. I saw Avi today.

—Who?

—My half brother.

—Oh right. The baby Avi.

—He's not a baby anymore. He's two.

—How was it?

—Sort of strange. I'd never seen him before.

—You never met him till today?

—No.

—How is he? Is he cute?

—I don't know.

—You don't know?

—No.

—All right.

—Eve tell me something.

—Yeah?

—Can you imagine what it feels like to have a father who doesn't want you?

I looked at her. —Can you imagine that feeling?

Eve stared at me silently. Then she said no.

After that I had to see Samantha. I longed to be with her again, back in the warm embrace of her family. That was my ticket to happiness, I was sure of it.

I called her at work. We had one of our coy back-and-forths. In a tone of feigned indifference I asked if she was seeing anyone.

—No. Not really, she said.

—Not really?

—No! she said, perhaps too emphatically.

I waited for her to say we should get together. She didn't.

—Maybe we should do something sometime, I said.

—All right. When?

Now I was the one forcing the issue. This was her power over me—the more elusive she was the more desperate I got.

—Anytime. I'm open. I have nothing going on.

—Let's see. What about next Thursday?

—Next Thursday's great.

I suggested Maz Mezcal. It was a calculated move. Maz Mezcal was one of our spots when we dated, scene of groovy times. I thought just being there with me would make her see she'd made a terrible mistake and that we were meant to be together.

We met at the restaurant and drank margaritas. The evening quickly assumed magical hues. We were finishing our entrees when her cellphone rang. She checked the display. Something changed in her face.

—Don't get it, I said.

—It'll just take a second, she said, putting the phone to her ear. —Hey. Not much, just having dinner with a friend. Maz Mezcal. No we're almost done. No it's on Eighty-sixth. Between First and Second. Huh? No why don't—why don't we—Hello? Hello?

She put the phone down.

—That was my friend Darnell.

—Who?

—Darnell. He's—meeting us for a drink.

—Meeting us where?

—Here.

—*Here?* He's coming here? When?

—Now.

—Well call him back and tell him not to come.

—We got cut off. I think he's just down the street.

—Who the fuck is Darnell?

—I tried to tell him—

—Can't you—wait, who the fuck is Darnell? Samantha?

I looked at her. She was looking past me. She smiled and waved. I became aware of a presence. I turned and glanced up at a dude maybe thirty, glasses, bald, paunch, blue button-up, khakis.

I turned away. Samantha still had that frozen fucking smile.

—Darnell this is Bryan.

He stuck a hand in my face. I shook it but didn't say anything or look up. Darnell may have said hey Bryan. He may have said nice to meet you.

I got up from the table and left the restaurant without a word. At Lexington I turned left and walked thirty or so blocks. I stopped at a pizza place and bought a bottled water. I saw myself in the mirrored wall under the fluorescent lights looking deranged. I pictured Samantha fucking Darnell, pictured the meaty paw he'd offered me squeezing her ass and tits, pictured Samantha doing things to Darnell that she'd once done to me. I didn't fight these images. I let them play out.

I hadn't left any money at the restaurant. We'd had all those margaritas—the bill must've been eighty dollars or more.

Fuck it. I was glad. Let that cocksucker Darnell pony up for my meal.

I left the pizza place and walked. I wanted every third woman I saw to take me home with her. I wanted to light myself on fire and run into the street.

I lay on the floor of my room in the dark. I held the phone to my ear and listened to Hasna. I hadn't seen her since our two brief encounters a year ago, first at the bar and then when she'd handed me off to her friend who took me to see Guided by Voices. Instead we talked on the phone. Every few months I would call her or she would call me and we'd talk for an hour, sometimes longer.

We always talked at night. There was an intimacy to our conversations, much more so than if we'd met at a bar or gone to a restaurant. I felt comfortable telling her things, like I'd known her for years. In a strange way she knew me as well or better than most people I'd met in New York. And I'd certainly never met anyone like her.

She was born in Detroit to Lebanese parents. They moved to Saudi Arabia when Hasna was one. A short time later they returned to the US. They moved back to Saudi in 1985 and stayed for five years. Within a few weeks of the Iraqi invasion of Kuwait her family—which now included six kids—was on a plane to the US. They resettled in Detroit when Hasna was thirteen.

I was attracted to her personality and my memory of what she looked like. Yet when it came to romance she issued conflicting vibes. She alluded to a few boys she'd made out with but told me that in each case she'd cut ties immediately. She was flirty and friendly but said the notion of a relationship gave her anxiety and that commitment probably wasn't for her. She was more interested in hearing about my fraught non-entanglements than in discussing her own. She laughed when I talked about freaking out around Jasmine. She sympathized when I told her the story of Samantha and Darnell.

She said it was probably time I reconciled with my father.

The oddest thing about our phone-only friendship was we were essentially neighbors. She could have walked over in fifteen minutes. Still, for some reason neither of us suggested getting together. Something about our arrangement worked.

Every so often I'd realize we hadn't talked in a while and figure we were on the verge of falling out of touch. Then some random night like tonight the phone would ring. It would be Hasna.

I'd turn out the lights and lie on the floor.

We'd talk till I couldn't go on anymore.

****

We loaded up the car topper and left Fair Lawn around dusk. Paul took the night shift, as is his custom, drove all night wearing headphones listening to music at a low volume. Trish slept in the passenger seat. We'd lowered the backseat and made a bed with some blankets and pillows. I lay back there with Barney. I took two Xanax, put *Under the Bushes Under the Stars* in my Discman, and faded away. When I woke it was daylight. We were at a Bob Evans somewhere. We ate breakfast and walked Barney behind the restaurant. We got back in the car. Now Paul slept in the back and Trish and I traded shifts. We arrived in Minneapolis after twenty hours of driving and checked into the hotel. We had just enough time to shower and change before getting in the car again and driving to Bits's uncle's house for the rehearsal dinner. I was a groomsman. Zoe introduced me to my counterpart. We ran through the ceremony. Several of our friends from the old days were there. We sat in the backyard eating, drinking, laughing, cycling through the same old stories and memories. It felt good to be sitting in a backyard in the suburbs on a cool evening holding a beer. The family had a dog named Ben. Ben had a wise air about him. I fell in love with Ben. I spent much time in the grass or on the living room floor speaking quietly to him and scratching his ears, searching his soulful eyes for some clue to existence. I couldn't recall meeting any human being recently who'd made me feel as good as old Ben. I was sad to leave him and go back to the hotel. The next day a bunch of us went to the Mall of America. I split off from the group. They went on rides and ate at the Cereal Adventure Cafe. I bought a new pair of sneakers and a Twins T-shirt. A few hours later I was standing with the others on a riser in the Minneapolis History Center and Bits and Zoe were married. The reception was in the Great Hall. A microphone was set up. I made a short speech but it was mostly lost in the big space. I drank beer after beer and my heart was full of love for my friends and for the goodness that still seemed possible in this beastly existence. After the reception everyone went to a bar but I went back to the hotel, changed my clothes, and walked Barney in the parking lot. It was a humid night and I was dehydrated, already slightly hungover. The next morning I found Paul passed out on the blankets in the car with the hatchback open and his legs hanging out. Trish and I roused him and we drove across town to a Red Roof Inn. We left Paul and Barney sleeping in the room, drove to the Metrodome, and watched the Twins beat the Tigers. We left the next morning at six, drove ten hours into Michigan's Upper Peninsula. We spent two days in Grand Marais in a cabin near Lake Superior. We took long walks through the woods and along the Pictured Rocks National Lakeshore. We drank strong microbrew beers made with water from Lake Superior and ate pizza at the Dune Saloon. On the Fourth of July we crossed into Canada and spent the night in a tent at a KOA campground. We hadn't brought air mattresses and the ground was cold and hard. The KOA store was ill-stocked. There were train tracks nearby and the trains were loud and kept us awake so the next day we drove to Barrie, Ontario and checked into a Travelodge. Paul walked into town looking for record stores. Trish and I tried to swim in the pool but they'd used too much chlorine and it burned our eyes and the fumes made us gag and we went back to the room and slept. We woke when Paul returned. He said the town was nice but he hadn't found any good record stores. We stayed in the room that night watching *The Brady Bunch*, eating a Little Caesar's pizza. I suggested we stay in Barrie for good but the next morning we left, went on through Canada, dropped down into New York. We stayed the night in Syracuse in a roach-infested apartment with old friends of Paul and Trish's. I passed out on the couch while everyone else stayed up drinking. The next day was Saturday. We drove back to the city. We rolled into Greenpoint after dark and they came up and we ordered Thai delivery from Amarin. Paul looked around and said it was crazy that I still lived in this apartment, it seemed like such a long time ago that we'd all moved to New York. Then they left and the trip was behind us. Sunday I woke late and spent the afternoon reading the *Times*. The next day the clock radio alarm went off at 6:40.

We sat in a windowless storage room going through boxes of give-away items, many of them branded with various iterations of the company name and logo. Billie and Sarah were organizing the clutter.

—This is fun, I said. —I like it in here.

—How is this fun? asked Sarah.

—I don't know. I just like it. It's cool. Sorta secret. It reminds me of this time we had a lock-in in high school. Everyone was supposed to just stay in the library but we ran around all over the school all night.

—A lock-in?

—A sleepover. It was for the literary club.

Sarah chuckled. —The literary club.

—Hey don't laugh. I was the founding president.

—And it served you well.

—That's what we should do here, have a lock-in.

—You wanna stay the night in this room? said Billie.

—Yeah. Just the three of us. Don't you think it'd be fun?

—B, you're crazy.

—We could do it tonight. We'll go home and get a change of clothes and come back and sneak in and stay the night here. Who would know?

—No one. Because we're not doin it.

—We could have sleeping bags and music. Hang around and talk. Go down and get a pizza from Sbarro for dinner.

—What about Ozzie? asked Sarah. Her eight-year-old son.

—Ozzie can come too. We'll go to the Battery Park theater and see a movie or something first. Don't you think Ozzie would dig it?

—Hell no.

Billie laughed. —I don't think it's gonna happen, B. As exciting as it sounds.

—Well we have to do *something*.

—Why?

—Because. Today's my birthday.

—Your birthday. For real?

—Yeah.

—Happy birthday, they said.

—Thank you.

—How old are you?

—Twenty-seven.

Sarah laughed. —And that's your big birthday plan, come up into this storeroom with a sleeping bag? What's wrong with you, boy?

—What about your friends? said Billie. —They're not taking you out?

—Not tonight.

—Someone should take you out on your birthday.

—Okay, I said. —Any ideas?

We went to the big theater on Forty-second Street and watched a movie called *The Score*. It starred Robert De Niro and Marlon Brando. Brando was fat, hideous, and lisping and the movie was bad. We ate dinner at Chevy's, a chain Mexican restaurant across the street. Chevy's was my kind of scene. Cavernous, corporate, at once overfriendly and profoundly impersonal. We sat in a huge booth eating chips and salsa, drinking neon margaritas with barely any tequila from fishbowl-size glasses. Billie and Sarah split the enchiladas. I ate chicken fajitas. When the check came they grabbed it and split it three ways. I ponied up the bread for my own birthday dinner and didn't mind at all. We walked out into Times Square. The drinks must have been alcoholic enough because standing on Forty-second Street I felt overwhelmed and happy and a little scared. I gazed with wonder at all the people and the big flashing signs.

This time he was in the next stall over and the unrolling was so intense it shook the wall between us. I stood and threw open the door and pretended to leave. For a moment or two he was quiet. I held my breath, didn't move a muscle. When he started again I slipped into another stall and sat on the toilet without undoing my pants. I sat there motionless for ten minutes or more. Finally the unrolling and flushing stopped. He waited another few minutes doing god knows what and then left the stall. I heard him at the sinks. Slowly I stood, took a breath, and walked out.

He worked in sales. He was fairly young, of average weight, slightly below-average height. I'd seen him countless times but hadn't met him before. He had dark close-cropped hair and vaguely simian features. I could tell by the look on his face that I'd surprised him and that it shamed him to be found out. We stood for a while at opposing rows of sinks, scrubbing our hands as if going into surgery. He left first.

I went to Whelan's desk and sat in the chair.

—I know who it is.

—Who?

—The toilet paper guy.

—You found out?

—Yes.

—Who is it?

I said I didn't know his name. I described him.

—That guy? said Whelan.

—You know him?

—Yeah. I mean no I don't know him but if it's the same guy I'm thinking he asked me to join a March Madness pool this year.

—He works in sales.

—Yeah. He came down here looking to sign people up.

—Short black hair. Sort of gumpy looking.

—Yeah.

—He never asked me to join any March Madness pool.

—Well he definitely came by. Maybe you weren't around.

—Do me a favor. Go down there and see if it's the same guy.

—I'm not going down there, said Whelan.

—Why wouldn't he ask me to join the March Madness pool?

—I don't know. Does it bother you?

—Yes. It bothers me.

—Why? He's insane. He stands in the bathroom shoving toilet paper everywhere.

—I like to be included.

—Maybe he'll come by next year.

—Maybe.

—How'd you figure it out anyway?

—I waited him out.

—What do you mean?

—I tricked him into thinking I'd left the men's room then snuck into a stall and sat on the toilet and waited till he finished.

—You're joking.

—No.

—You ran a sting operation?

—Yes.

—Okay so who's more disturbed? You or this guy?

—That's a good question. Apparently he got enough of a bad vibe that he didn't ask me to join the March Madness pool.

—Did you tell Frank and Patrick?

—No. I'm gonna go tell them now.

—Good work, he said.

—Thank you.

It was Saturday afternoon. The phone rang.

—Baines, I said.

—How you doing, man?

—Good. It's good to hear from you. Are you back in town?

—Yeah I just got back.

—How does it feel?

—Reentry's tough. New York is a fucking pit.

He said classes began soon and asked when I was starting up. A couple of weeks, I said. We talked for a while about other things and then he said it was tough, he had a lot of shit going on, he was trying to get a story in shape for publication.

—That's great, I said. —Where?

—The *Paris Review*.

Something inside me dropped. I held it together.

—That's great. Congratulations.

—Thanks.

—How'd that come about?

—I just sent it in.

—You, not your agent?

—No. I just put it in an envelope and sent it off.

—Which story?

—"North Star."

I'd read a few drafts of "North Star." I remembered I'd spent a morning at my desk giving it a thorough going-over at his request.

—It was strange, he said. —I mean one day I'm sitting there and I get a phone call and they patch me through to George Plimpton.

—What did he say?

—Not much. He gave me his edits. They were slight, just a line or two. I hung up thinking, man, I don't know.

—What?

—How could they want to publish this story that's so clearly full of holes?

—Meaning your story?

—Yeah. You read it.

—Yes I did.

—It needs work.

We talked some more. Baines recommended reading *Eleven Kinds of Loneliness* by Richard Yates. He said they'd just published Yates's collected stories and I should check that out. We made plans to get together next week and hung up.

I sat on the couch for a while. Then I got up and went into the bathroom. I stared at myself in the mirror. You're a fucking failure, I said. Tears filled my eyes and spilled out. You're a fucking failure. My face grew red and hot. Hot tears poured down. You're a fucking failure. I said it over and over. I spat at my blurred crying face. You're a fucking failure. I spat again. I walked into the living room, lay on the floor, and cried.

After a while I stopped. I washed my face with cold water and left the apartment. I passed McCarren Park and looked at all the couples lying on blankets in the grass. I took the L to Eighth Avenue, the end of the line, but didn't get off. The train left the station heading back into Brooklyn. At Graham Avenue I got out, walked to a payphone, and called Erin. She answered and I asked if I could come over.

—Where are you? she said.

—At the end of the block.

She opened the door, saw my face, and asked what was wrong. We went upstairs to her room. I sat in the chair and she sat on the bed. I told her Baines was publishing a story in the *Paris Review*. She came over and hugged me.

—I've worked so hard and nothing happens I keep getting rejected everything I write gets rejected everything happens for Baines I don't know what to do you should've heard him oh I don't know why they want to publish my story it's so full of holes but I guess if they want it they can have it whatever Erin I don't know what to do.

—It'll be okay, Bryan.

—No it won't.

—Yes it will. Trust me.

Two days later I sat in my cubicle thinking. I opened a new e-mail and addressed it to Baines. I wrote that I couldn't meet up with him, I was too jealous. I said I knew it made me look bad but it was too hard for me to watch him achieve with ease things I'd worked so long and futilely for. I said big things were going to happen for him and I couldn't listen to him wonder why people wanted to publish him and tell me his stories were full of holes. I said I was sorry and hoped he understood.

I sat with the message open on the screen a long time. I reread it, changed a few things, and clicked send. I felt like a fucking baby. I felt like a piece of shit. I also felt strangely liberated and took perverse delight in having told the truth.

Later that day Baines wrote back. I stared at his name in my inbox imagining all the things his message might say. I decided I didn't want to know. I deleted it without reading it. Then I went into the trash and deleted it permanently.

The following week I was sitting in my room in Galesburg listening to the sound of the rain and my uncle Art playing guitar in the living room. I drove to Meijer's and aimlessly walked the aisles. It felt good knowing that no one I saw cared if Baines got published in the *Paris Review* or if anyone did, and that of all the people in Meijer's at that moment I was likely the only one who even knew what the *Paris Review* was.

Ed grilled burgers for dinner and we sat on the porch later, drinking coffee and eating cookies and looking out at the wet swamp.

I fell asleep with the fan on and cool air coming in, listening to the insects in the misty night. I dreamed I was making out with Gwyneth Paltrow. I asked if she'd go on a date with me. Yes, she said, but only because you want it so much more than I do. I got mad, pushed her away, and told her forget it.

Saturday night I went to Harvey's and ran into a few old friends. I walked over to the Blue Dolphin and was standing outside when it started to rain. I huddled with some other people under an awning. We watched the rain soak Kalamazoo. I missed this city and loved it so much and couldn't wait to get back for Christmas.

But as it turned out I came home much sooner than that.

Sunday afternoon, 9/2/01.

I pushed through the turnstile and entered the concourse, feeling strange in my old Today's Man suit. I entered the One World Trade lobby and rode the elevators to Windows on the World. Milton, Doreen, and Dana were there. Mattie, Max, and Frank were there, as were Lois and Shirley. We went into the main room and took our seats with the other guests. Ward stood there waiting. Ginny came beaming down the aisle. The ceremony was simple and brief.

I thought of interviewing with Ginny all those months ago. I remembered commenting on her James Dean photo and the view from her office. I wouldn't have guessed I'd be attending her wedding, or her father's funeral for that matter, which I'd done last fall. I wouldn't have guessed she'd come to think of me as a friend.

At dinner I sat with Milton, Dana, Doreen, and her husband. The sun had set. The city sparkled a thousand feet below. The band began playing. Ginny and Ward had their first dance. Slowly other people trickled onto the dance floor. After a few fast numbers a slow song came on. Doreen and Kyle went out there. I was thinking of asking Dana when I saw Lois had risen and was coming this way.

—Bryan would you care to dance?

—Certainly.

We walked onto the dance floor. I put my arm around her waist. She placed her hand in mine. We began to move.

—I gotta tell you, Lois. I'm a little nervous.

—Oh don't be, she said. —I'm just another girl.

Whenever we passed Frank and Max's table I could see them grinning and then when Lois's back was turned, laughing. Frank came over with one of the disposable cameras that had been left at each place-setting. He snapped a few pictures.

—For the bulletin board, he said.

I smiled. We danced. The song we'd begun dancing to blended into another slow number. I realized with alarm the band was playing a medley. Lois and I went around and around the dance floor. We'd talked briefly at first. Now there was nothing to say. The medley continued. Lois and I danced, her shiny pink mouth just inches away from my face. At last it ended. I walked to the table and gulped wine. Frank came over.

—Get some nice shots? I said.

He laughed. —I think you just locked up a good bonus.

You think you've got something good but you're never quite sure. You can't trust your initial judgment. Especially if it comes in that warm wave of good feeling just after you've finished. I thought I'd written good stories before. Stories of strong feeling with sharply drawn characters doing and saying interesting things. I'd thought this many times but no editor had ever agreed with me enough to publish one. They may have half-ass agreed in a few written comments on a rejection note. But if they really thought what you'd sent was that promising wouldn't their impulse be to work with you on it to help make it better and then publish it? So you see, you can never be sure.

This time I was sure.

The story had come quickly. I'm not a fast writer so this was a promising sign. I'd written about maybe or maybe not losing my virginity to an older girl in a house on West Main and had woven it in with an earlier story—"Scars," the first story I'd written in New York—about meeting a girl with scars on her arms who told me *Naked Lunch* was her bible. In the new story the older girl was named Trudy. The girl with the scars was Helene. The main character was essentially me. I'd written the new material in a single afternoon, titled the piece "My Hideous Bride," and because I was so sure it was good, I volunteered to go first in my first fiction workshop.

I sat low in a bucket seat while the class discussed it. The experience was like what I remembered from undergrad: a bunch of people said things and then other people said contradictory things back.

I was told the voice of the story was funny and compelling and also that it was a little too flip. I was told to make the character of Trudy more physically unappealing and that that wasn't necessary, the point was clear. I was told the absentee father stuff was interesting but maybe there should be more about the mother in there too. I was told "My Hideous Bride" was a good title and that something about it didn't quite feel earned. I wrote notes and kept my face blank. The teacher, Irini, gave her comments last. She said among other things that she liked the voice and the characters in the story and that she saw it as being a part of something longer. She asked if I'd considered using any of this material for a novel. Yes, I said, I mean kind of, I mean I've just started to think in those terms. It wasn't true. I'd never seriously considered writing a novel. Maybe I thought I would someday but it would have to be a day far in the future, when I had more time and knew more what I was doing and had something more interesting to say.

I walked out to the quad. It had been a long day. I was tired but felt better than I had in months. For the last couple hours I'd been a writer—not a financial copywriter who dreamed of being a writer.

The quad was pretty. There were trees and grass. It didn't look like you were in the city at all. Fall was coming, my favorite time of year. It was a beautiful time and I was a writer.

I took the train part of the way home then got out at Eastern Parkway and boarded the B48. It lumbered slowly north. I read through the written comments the class had returned to me. There was one note I kept looking at, one I'd written myself, a single word on a page cluttered with scrawled marks: *Novel?*

Four nights later I sat in a book-lined study in a house unlike any other I'd seen in New York. It had three stories, a front porch, and appeared to have many rooms. It was deep in Brooklyn in a neighborhood I'd never heard of. The block was lined with similar houses, all of them large and unattached.

The study smelled pleasantly of dusty books. On one end was a desk with a banker's lamp on it. In front of the desk was a window looking out at the sidewalk and the street. I was sitting on the other end of the room by the books. Across from me sat a man with a beard and a penetrating blue-eyed gaze. He held one of my stories in his lap, "Blueberry Pancakes." We'd discussed it briefly when I first arrived. Then we'd talked at length about sports. The man was a Mets fan. His knowledge of the franchise was staggering. He touched on current and former players, stats, team low points, momentous victories. I told him Derek Jeter was from my hometown of Kalamazoo. He said rooting for the Yankees was like rooting for the Republican Party. I said I didn't root for them necessarily but had come to admire their team-play approach. Brosius, Williams, Martinez, O'Neill—these weren't your typical marquee names but they'd ground it out and gotten it done. The man predicted those days were ending. The Yankees were poised to win another World Series but look for Jason Giambi to start at first base next year. Giambi? I couldn't see it. Martinez was beloved. Giambi was a hulking party boy. We'll see, said the man. We moved on to basketball. He was equally knowledgeable about the Knicks. The talk moved beyond me. I struggled to keep up. I began to have to urinate and squirmed in my chair. As we were wrapping up I thought of asking to use the bathroom. But I hesitated and missed my window and then I was out on the street.

I stood at the end of the outdoor subway platform and thought of pissing on the tracks. Then I thought maybe there was a camera somewhere. The person in the booth could see me and call the cops. I decided to hold it. I rode all the way through Brooklyn back into Manhattan and transferred to the L at Union Square. I got out at Graham Avenue and rushed to Erin's. I pounded on the door. She came down.

—Thank god you're home.
—Why, what's up?
—Can I use your bathroom?
She smiled and shook her head.
—You really know how to sweep a girl off her feet.

I came out of the bathroom sighing deeply with relief. Erin was at the stove stirring something in a pan.
—You want some soup?
—No thanks.
She poured soup in a bowl. She sat and ate.

—I don't get you, she said.

—What?

—Why didn't you just ask the guy to use the bathroom?

—I don't know. For some reason I just couldn't.

—He's your teacher?

—Yeah.

—Why'd you go to his house?

—That's where he wanted to meet.

—And it's just the two of you?

—Yeah. It's a one-on-one tutorial. Maybe that's the thing that made me feel strange. We spent most of the time talking about sports.

—Sports?

—Baseball. Basketball.

—You didn't talk about your story?

—A little.

—Next time ask to use the bathroom, Bryan. Don't be afraid.

She finished her soup and put the bowl in the sink. We went into her room. A few minutes later it started to rain. I looked out at the rain falling hard in the street. As soon as it lets up I'll get going, I thought.

Erin was lying on the bed. I fell down next to her. The sound of the rain was soothing. The wet air smelled good. The room was lit by a single lamp. The vibe in the room changed. I kissed her. We kissed softly at first then with greater urgency.

It was happening again. Another last time.

Afterward we lay in each other's arms. The rain tapered off. I got out of bed and got dressed. Erin put on a robe. I sat next to her and kissed her. We talked for a minute. I said goodbye and left. The streets were empty and quiet and wet.

Back in my apartment I was wide awake, nervous. I lay in the dark with my eyes closed, listening to the air conditioner and the fan. It was late. I tried to trick myself into getting tired enough to sleep but the TV in the next apartment was loud and I was thinking about Erin and feeling guilty. I got out of bed and went to the kitchen. I filled a glass with tap water and took a Xanax. I went back to bed but the TV was still loud and I was still feeling crazy and still couldn't sleep. I looked at the clock. In just a few hours the alarm would go off. I closed my eyes, still buzzing. Sometime later I drifted off.

Don't Look Up

The clock radio alarm went off at 6:40. My eyes were dry. I was very thirsty. The Xanax was working. My limbs and head were heavy, I felt chained to the bed. As I listened to Howard Stern I thought about calling in sick. I decided against it—Ginny was still out on her honeymoon, the department was in panic mode, I didn't want it to seem like I was slacking off in her absence. I threw back the covers and got out of bed. I showered and dressed and went into the kitchen. I opened the fire escape window and leaned out. I stood for a moment taking in the bright day. I closed and locked the window and left the apartment. On the bus and the trains I read *Heavier Than Heaven*, a new biography of Kurt Cobain. It was hugely depressing. Cobain was portrayed as a desperate and out-of-control junkie, shooting up in seedy motels and in the back of his car. I was glad I hadn't known any of this when I was seventeen, the height of my fandom a decade ago. I walked through the concourse and took the elevator to forty-four. I stopped in the cafeteria for a coffee and a bagel. Up on seventy I continued reading. A few minutes later Whelan arrived. He sat at his desk, pressed some keys, clicked the mouse. You're in early, I said. I have to be at that stupid class at nine, he said. He meant Feedbacking Your Peers, part of a new Morgan Stanley initiative, a peer-review system where you would anonymously evaluate your coworkers and they in turn would evaluate you. The class was supposed to teach you how to write thoughtful, objective comments your colleagues could learn from. A rolling schedule had been established. Attendance was mandatory. Checking my e-mail I remembered I was taking the class today too. After Whelan settled in the office was quiet. I returned to my book. I took a bite of bagel with peanut butter and a sip of coffee. I liked to sip coffee right after and mix the salty and sweet and bitter flavors in my mouth. I looked at the clock in my desk phone—8:45. I was nearing the end of the book and thought I could finish before nine. If not I'd keep reading. No one would tell me to stop. A moment later I heard a noise or a series of noises, loud booms. The floor trembled. I looked up. An image came to me of a giant crane tipping over. Was there construction on one of the towers and I hadn't noticed? No, this was closer. It must be happening down the hall because Cal Leonard, a guy in accounting who had the office next to Frank's, was now yelling and wouldn't stop. OH MY GOD. OH DEAR GOD. OH MY GOD. OH GOD. I got a strange feeling and stood up. Another image came to me of a row of filing cabinets falling over. One of those big banks of filing cabinets fell over and crushed someone, I thought. Cal Leonard was still yelling. Whelan and Max were standing by Sylvia's office staring out. I walked over and stood next to them. All I could see through the window were thousands of papers flying around. Some of the papers were burning. Hey, said Max, that building's on fire. Whelan and I walked over to Ginny's office and looked out. The papers were coming down in a wild flurry with orange flames on the burned ones and also a kind of thin gray haze. I went to my desk and grabbed my backpack. I walked to the hall by the elevators. A crowd had already formed there. People were shouting questions. The security guard was just standing up from his desk. What's that now, he said, something happened to the other building? We stood there waiting. No one knew what had happened. I looked around at the group. Everyone I saw looked scared. I thought of Cal Leonard's screams. We waited for an announcement. No announcement came. Someone said shit the fire warden's not here, where the fuck is the fire warden? More people arrived. The area was jammed. Sarah was there, holding on to Blanca, her boss. Blanca was crying and wiping at her tears but more kept coming. Whelan asked if I'd seen Lila. I said no. He went to look for her and came back alone. She must not be in yet, he said. A few minutes passed. People argued about what to do. Some said evacuate. Others said wait. Some headed for the elevators. Others said no, if we're gonna leave we should take the stairs. I was scared. I couldn't talk. I wanted someone official to get on the intercom and say what was happening. Confusion mounted. I couldn't make a decision. It was made for me. A door to a stairwell opened. It was packed with workers from higher floors already making their way down. Traffic was two-lane, shoulder to shoulder. I waited my turn. I looked at the little plate by the door that said 70 and took my first step. A woman from sales named Sue was next to me. Sue radiated ease and composure. Are you scared, Bryan? she said. I told her I was. I've never seen you like this, she said, usually you always have something to say. We walked down a few flights. Sue fell back. Whelan appeared on my right. I heard people talking. They said a plane hit the other tower. Details beyond that were vague. A woman behind me was saying she'd seen people jumping out of windows. I turned and looked at her. Her face was red from crying. Her eyes were crazy. She didn't seem to see me. Descent was slow. We'd gone about ten floors. The loudspeaker crackled. The line slowed and then stopped. BE QUIET. HOLD UP. LISTEN. LISTEN. SHUT UP. There is a problem in building one, said a voice. Building two is secure. I repeat. Building two is secure. Please return to your desks and await further instruction. The voice repeated this message but didn't specify the problem. But the voice was official and I was vaguely relieved. The mood in the stairwell lightened. A guy in front of me said fuck it, I'm walkin back up. He brushed by me and was gone. I turned to Whelan. What do you think? I don't know, what do you think? he said. I paused for a second. Let's check it out. All right, he said. We walked to the next exit and got out of the stairwell. We were on some strange floor in the fifties. All the walls were white. I didn't see any offices. People crowded the halls. They all looked scared. They laid out possible next moves in voices pitched near total panic. The mood on the floor seemed at odds with what the voice on the speaker had said. A man walked by us shaking his head. He said bodies were falling out of the other building by the dozen. Some other guys heard this and ran to go see. My feeling of relief vanished. Whelan this is insane, let's get the fuck out of here, I said. Whelan agreed. We got back in the stairwell. We kept going down. A moment later huge sound erupted. The building shook. I slipped down the stairs. I grabbed the railing. The tower pitched forward. The tower groaned. Then it stopped and rocked back in the other direction. The huge sound was still happening and then it wasn't anymore. People around me cried out for god. The tower swayed. It felt like it was going to break in two and fall into the street. My mind switched off. I didn't start praying. I didn't have visions of childhood. My life didn't flash before my eyes. It was a puzzling feeling. I was cold inside. Here it comes, I thought, get ready. A moment later I was still alive. The building was still swaying but I was able to stand. What the fuck is happening, Whelan? Are we being bombed? No, he said, that was just the fuel tank from the plane exploding in the other tower. The fuel tank. It seemed reasonable. And Whelan had said it with such confidence. The stairwell was hot and smelled of smoke. I looked again at Whelan. His face was ashen. He was staring at a woman ahead of us. She was fat and moved slowly, heaving her body back and forth. She was shoeless and babbling an endless prayer. *Oh please god oh please lord oh please god oh please lord.* I felt a need to touch people. I squeezed Whelan's shoulder. The woman behind me was sobbing. I turned around and squeezed her shoulder. I ran my hand down her back over her sweat-soaked shirt. I smiled at the man next to her and shook his hand. It's gonna be okay, I called out almost involuntarily. I didn't believe this but kept saying it anyway. Sometimes the line stopped cold. We'd stand there immobile. Voices above us screaming NO DON'T STOP GO DOWN KEEP MOVING. I kept track of the floor numbers. Forty. Wait. Thirty-seven. Wait. Thirty-two. Wait. I wasn't wearing a watch. I didn't know how long we'd been in there. My only frame of reference was floor numbers. Floor numbers were my life. I ticked them off slowly. Then we wound down the last ten floors. We exited the stairwell on the mezzanine level. Police and rescue workers were there shouting instructions. They kept us moving in a line. We moved past the big windows. The plaza was filled with burning metal and smoke and ash. I didn't understand what I was seeing out there. We waited in a long line at the inoperable escalator. We walked down to the lobby and into the dark mall. All the stores were empty. There was water on the ground and broken glass in the water. We walked by Banana Republic and turned left at J. Crew. Whelan and I shook hands. He gripped my shoulder. You're pretty cool under pressure there, Bry, he said. We turned right at Sbarro and waited in another long line. A series of banners was visible featuring cartoon twin towers inside a shopping bag over the words SHOP THE WORLD. I walked up the escalator toward Borders. Cops hustled us along. They shouted at everyone to turn off their cellphones. DO NOT LOOK UP. WHATEVER YOU DO, DO NOT LOOK UP. JUST KEEP MOVING. DO NOT LOOK UP. I stepped through the door into the light of day. A man yelled through a bullhorn. DON'T STOP. GO UP FULTON TO BROADWAY. The air smelled of acrid smoke. Debris blanketed the pavement. Ash floated down. Sirens blared. I felt the pull of whatever was behind me.

I turned around and looked up.

Blood was splattered in Church Street. It shone bright red in the dust. I kept looking back, staring over my shoulder. I tried to square what I was seeing with what I'd heard in the stairwell about a plane. It didn't add up. A man with a spiral notebook approached me.

—Hey buddy, were you in there, would you talk to me? he said.

I shook my head and waved him off. The guy behind me started telling his story.

I walked up Fulton Street. I kept looking back.

People lined Broadway staring up at the buildings. Whelan was gone. I was alone in the crowd. I couldn't stop staring at the towers. I seemed to be leaving my body. I felt very light.

Jenny spotted me. She was with Sue. Jenny urged me to join them. The three of us went north. We lost Sue at Vesey Street. Fire trucks passed. Jenny and I walked a little farther. We stopped at City Hall. I asked what she wanted to do. She said she just wanted to get away from here. Her dad worked in the city, way uptown, West End Avenue and Sixty-fifth. I'll go with you, I said.

We saw a woman with a cellphone. Jenny asked if she could use it.

—Yeah you can try, said the woman, —but all the circuits are jammed.

Jenny pressed some buttons. Nothing happened. She gave back the phone. The woman smiled and said good luck.

I was staring at the towers. I wanted to pause and try to figure this shit out. Jenny insisted we keep going.

We walked to Canal Street and headed east. The sidewalks were mobbed. We stopped at a double-sided pay phone and waited. Jenny stood in one line, I stood in the other. A woman in front of me was speaking Chinese into the receiver. She was taking a long time. She wasn't crying and didn't appear to be panicked. Jenny was on the other phone now, tears on her face. I tapped the woman on the shoulder. I told her I'd just been in the World Trade Center and I needed to use the phone right now. The woman glared at me, spoke some more, hung up.

I took out my credit card and punched in the numbers. The signal died. I couldn't concentrate. I had no idea what to do next. Jenny appeared, took my card, and dialed.

The call went through. My mother answered.

—Hello, she said, her voice very grave.

—Hi mom, I said.

She started sobbing.

—Honey! she cried. —Honey it's Bryan!

Ed got on the phone, started to talk and then stopped.

—Hello? Are you there?

—Yeah I'm here. I love you, Brain.

None of this reached me. I couldn't react. I was still in the cold place I'd entered back in the stairwell. My mom came on again. I said I had to go, there were other people waiting to use the phone.

We cut up some side streets and stopped at a deli. Jenny bought a water. I stared into the cooler and contemplated buying a beer.

We walked up Lafayette Street through Astor Place. We took a left at some point. Two women approached Jenny asking for directions to West Fourth Street. I stood in the middle of Fifth Avenue looking south. One World Trade Center burned in the distance.

A moment later it fell.

People in the street cried out. I reached for Jenny's hand, held it a moment, let go. I heard a click. A woman had just taken my picture. I assumed Two World Trade — my building — was hidden in the smoke. I turned to a woman next to me.

—The other building's still there, right?

She shook her head. —No. They're both gone.

We stopped at an AT&T store across from Madison Square Park. Jenny explained our situation and asked if we could use the phone. She went first. I went to the bathroom and pissed. I stood in the back of the store looking out at the street. An AT&T guy told me the Supreme Court had been destroyed.

Jenny hung up. I walked to the counter and called Erin. She heard my voice and started to cry.

—I didn't die in that bullshit, I said.

Erin was crying and said nothing.

—Fuck this shit. I can't live here anymore. I can't live in a place where something like this can happen. I'm getting the fuck out of here. I'm leaving.

—When?

—As soon as possible. Right fucking now.

I told her I'd call back. I hung up and dialed Paul and Trish. Paul answered on the first ring. He said they were going nuts, they'd been trying to reach me all morning. I said I wanted to try and get out there somehow, keep the line open, I'll call back in a while.

I sat in Jenny's dad's office watching TV. A 767 struck Two World Trade Center repeatedly from multiple angles. I could still hear the explosion and feel the building sway. Two World Trade collapsed. One World Trade followed. I watched them disintegrate again and again. I pieced together a loose chronology. Smoke pours from the north tower. People jump or fall out of windows. A plane enters the frame. Two World Trade explodes. Both towers burn.

Both disappear. My building fell first. I wondered how long I'd been out. It couldn't have been long. I watched the images on a loop. I wondered how many people were dead. I wondered if anyone I knew was dead. Jenny and her dad returned from the cafeteria with lunch.

Jenny's dad was driving a coworker to Hackensack. I mentioned my friends in New Jersey. He said he'd drop me in Fair Lawn. We drove uptown through surprisingly thin traffic. The radio was tuned to 1010 WINS. Giuliani was on the air urging everyone to remain calm. No one in the car spoke. On the George Washington Bridge we all turned to the left. The southern end of Manhattan was shrouded in smoke.

Paul and Trish met me in the driveway. Jenny and I exchanged numbers. She and her dad drove off. We walked up the back steps and into the apartment. I sat on the couch. Barney came over. I gave him some pets and kissed his nose. His orange fur felt amazing. He had these little spiral curls on the back of his neck.
   —Barney I never thought I'd see you again.
   The TV was on. A plane hit my building. My building collapsed.
   Paul and Trish stood watching me. Trish finally spoke.
   —So . . . what happened?
   For the first time I started telling the story.

Paul lent me some shorts, a T-shirt, and one of the Youth Stream cellphones. We took Barney for a walk. I let them walk ahead of me and dialed my home number, waiting to hear my voice on the outgoing greeting. Instead a computer voice told me the answering machine was full. I dialed again and punched in my code. The computer voice told me I had thirty-five messages. It began with Erin. The call waiting beeped instantly. She sounded concerned but not hysterical. She said she really hoped I didn't go to work today. The call waiting beeped. The line clicked. The messages continued, interrupted every few seconds by call waiting. It was an odd series of voices. Some of these people I hadn't talked to in years.

The tone of the messages changed as the minutes passed. Urgency escalated. Everyone knew what was happening, knew it wasn't a freak accident, knew more than I did in the stairwell, which was almost nothing.

Erin called again and said please pick up if I was there. She said she loved me. She spoke through gasps and sobs and call waiting. I assumed the south tower had now fallen. Some of my friends thought they were addressing a dead man.

We drove to the ShopRite and loaded up on beer. We drove to the liquor store and bought tequila. Trish made margaritas. I'd given my mom the number here and now the phone rang nonstop. My e-mail inbox was flooded. There was a long thread of messages from Morgan Stanley people, asking for updates and contact info. As far as I could tell all my coworkers were fine. We kept the TV on. I couldn't stop watching. Every time the plane hit the building or the buildings collapsed I got a fresh jolt. We ordered an eggplant pizza for dinner. It was the best thing I'd ever tasted in my life.

I found Whelan's parents' number on one of the contact lists. His mother answered and I said who it was.

—Oh Bryan it's good to hear from you, thank god you're okay, I'm, I'm so grateful you were there with Brian, that the two of you had each other, knowing Brian had a friend with him through that means, it just means so much.

—I was glad he was there with me.

Whelan got on the line. He sketched out his day. He lost me in the madness outside and had no idea what to do next but wasn't about to stick around downtown. He walked across the Brooklyn Bridge, made his way to Atlantic Avenue, walked to the LIRR, caught a train out to Babylon.

—I met up with Jenny on Broadway. We walked to her dad's office.

—In Manhattan?

—Yeah. Way uptown. West End Avenue and Sixty-fifth.

—Jesus. How long did that take?

—I don't know. A long fucking time. Jenny's heels were bleeding.

—Well that's gotta be what, three or four miles?

—More than that. Five or six.

—We're at war. You realize that, right?

—I don't know. I guess so.

—Can you believe we were there?

—No I really can't. I see the plane coming in smashing into the building and that fireball and . . . I don't know. No. I can't believe it.

—How many people do you think were in there?

—Some people are saying ten thousand.

—Ten thousand people, he said.

—They told us to go back to our desks, remember that?

—Yes.

—On whose fucking instruction was that order given?

—I don't know. Whoever it was may not even be alive anymore.

—Remember what you said to me in the stairwell?

—When?

—When we heard that explosion?

—No. What'd I say?

—You said, I asked if we were being bombed and you said no, that was just the fuel tank from the plane blowing up in the other tower.

Whelan laughed. —The fuel tank.

I laughed. —Hey it sounded good. I believed it.

—Never mind that the whole building pitched.

We laughed.

—Let me ask you, said Whelan.

—Yeah?

—When you felt that. When you felt the building . . . move like that. Did you think you were going to die?

—Yes. I did.

—Me too, he said.

We started to laugh. We laughed a long time.

Sarah was at home in Brooklyn. She'd walked there and picked up Ozzie from school. She told me Billie was okay. Billie had been outside when the first plane hit and never made it inside.

—Oh my god, B, the air smells so bad. You can't escape it.

—You should come out to Fair Lawn.

—My back is killing me. I think I did something to it.

—We should have a big party. You and Billie should come out here.

—B, it is so awful. Everything smells burned.

—I saw you in the stairwell. You had your arm around Blanca.

—Blanca was a mess. It was like right away she was crying.

—You kept it together pretty well.

—Yeah but when I felt that explosion I prayed.

—Yeah?

—Oh yeah. I swear walking down those stairs and then all the way here messed up my back somehow. I can't even move from this chair.

—How's Ozzie?

—He's fine. He was scared for a while. He saw me and he ran to me when I walked through that door.

—I bet.

—B, nobody's heard from Tom Swift.

—What?

—Did you see him when we were up on the floor?

—I don't know. I don't remember. Tom Swift?

—Did you see him anywhere?

I tried to think. I couldn't remember.

—Tom Swift?

—Nobody's seen him. Nobody's heard from him.

I didn't want to call Lois. She'd already heard secondhand I was all right. Paul said maybe I should call her anyway, just as a courtesy. I sat on the floor and dialed. She launched at once into the tale of her morning. She'd been running late. She hailed a cab. She was en route from the Upper East Side when it happened. She said we needed to get the department up and running ASAP. She said there might be a group conference call tomorrow or maybe the day after, just to touch base and see where everyone stood. At some point they'd assign us to interim offices. Our file room and computers were gone obviously but our work was backed up on servers somewhere. But don't worry about that yet, she said, take some time, try to process what's happened, I'll send an e-mail about the conference call.

She circled back to her horror, her disbelief.

—Thank god the executives got out, she said.

We watched TV till late that night. It was the first time I could remember there being no commercials. I went up to the spare bedroom and turned on the AC. Paul and Trish tucked me in. Trish kissed my cheek. They said they were happy I was still alive. I said I was too. They turned off the light and closed the door. I lay in the dark for a few moments, thinking. Then I closed my eyes and immediately passed out.

My Life, Hit It

Another pretty morning. Fair Lawn was quiet. The school by the tennis courts was empty—no classes today. Paul and Trish walked out and began playing. I sat courtside and watched. It was funny to see them do something sporty but they weren't half bad. Their game progressed randomly. No one kept score. Tennis was a new thing with them. They'd found the racquets at a yard sale. I'd only played once, in freshman year gym class. Maybe played is the wrong word. I bashed every serve back over the high chain-link fence into the parking lot or the trees. I ogled girls in their gym gear, zeroing in on tit-bounce when they ran.

—You wanna play? said Paul.

—I don't know how.

—Neither do we, said Trish.

—You just kinda try and hit it back and forth.

—Nah you guys are good. You had some sweet volleys.

—I bet you'll be better than you think.

—Come on. You know me. You know I can't even throw.

—This is different, there's no throwing. Try it.

Paul gave me the racquet. I stuffed a couple tennis balls in my pocket. I stood on the baseline and looked over at Trish.

—Okay what do I do?

—You've seen tennis. Just throw it up and hit it.

—Don't think of it as throwing, said Paul. —Think of it as you toss the ball up.

I threw the ball up and swung. It cleared the net. Trish returned it. I knocked it back. She whiffed into the net.

—See, said Paul.

Trish tossed me the ball. I served again. We got a volley going. I played badly but Paul was right—I wasn't the embarrassment I thought I'd be.

The sun was bright. The day was warming. It felt good to be sweating. It felt good to move and lunge and yell *fuck* when I fucked something up. Trish called out made-up scores. I did my best McEnroe, threw down my racquet, yelled *You cannot—be serious!* My chest heaved and burned. It felt good to be winded. Sweat dripped down my face and stung my eyes and soaked through my shirt. I sniffed my armpit. It smelled bad. I smelled it again. I fell to the court spread-eagle and stared up at the sky. Trish walked over.

—Ready to take a break?

—Yeah. Who won?

—You did. Today's your special day.

I laughed. I caught my breath and rolled onto my feet. I walked over and checked the phone for missed calls. I dialed Sarah's number.

—Hey baby, she said.

—You know what I'm doing right now?

—What?

—Playing motherfucking tennis.

—Tennis?

—Yeah. I've never played before. I just played my first game.

—How was it?

—I think I'm pretty fucking good.

—Did you talk to Billie?

—No not yet. I'll call her next. Listen. Why don't you come out here.

—I can't. Ozzie and I are going to Atlanta.

—When, today?

—No but soon. I wanna see my family.

—How are you getting to Atlanta? You're not gonna fly.

—Oh my god no. We're taking the bus.

—The bus. That'll take three fucking days. No. What you should do is take a one-hour train ride into the great state of New Jersey.

—Yeah and do what? Play tennis?

—No. Have a big fucking party. Groove on each other. Love one another.

She laughed. —You're nuts, B.

—No I'm not, I'm real. I'm out here under the sun and the sky on this beautiful day and I'm fucking alive. You're alive. Can you feel it?

She laughed. —I can feel it.

—No baby say it louder. CAN YOU FEEL IT?

I was euphoric, walking in circles. I felt my heart pounding. I couldn't direct the flow of my thoughts. We hung up. Paul and Trish had a game going. I watched for a while then stood and stretched.

—You think the bagel place is open?

Max sent a group e-mail confirming that Tom Swift and Chris Grady—Denise's brother—were missing. I'd known about Tom but not about Chris Grady. I knew Denise vaguely. She worked in sales. Apparently her brother had worked in the north tower. Max's e-mail included contact info for Denise and Tom's wife Jan. He encouraged us to reach out to them but stressed that at this point Tom and Chris were officially missing, not yet presumed dead. There were other e-mails about the department-wide conference call. A time had been established, a dial-in number set up. I deleted these messages without writing anything down. I saved the one about Tom and Chris.

I was standing in a field not far from the tennis courts. I was talking to Peter on the phone about the scene at First Investors.

—Everyone was in my office listening to the radio, he said. —This is after the second plane hit. And we get this e-mail from Clara saying I see from the status list you guys have been busy, why don't we get together at ten and see where we are.

—Wait, ten a.m. yesterday?

—Yes.

—She called a meeting for ten a.m. yesterday—*after* the second plane hit?

—That's right.

—Fucking Clara. Although I must say I'm not shocked.

—Everyone deals with trauma differently.

I laughed. —Did anyone go to the meeting?

—She ended up rescheduling.

—Well let me know how it goes. I'm sure that bonds piece I started two years ago is still floating around.

—You could come right back and pick up where you left off.

—I'll pass.

—Have they mentioned where you'll be working now?

—No. There was some kind of conference call today but I didn't call in.

I told him I'd see him back in the city. I ended the call and stood holding the phone. I saw my friends in the distance and began walking toward them. Barney's tongue wagged. Barney was old now. Paul had picked him out of a box of puppies in front of the Petoskey Kmart in 1989. I'd known Barney almost as long as I'd known Paul.

I could see Paul and Trish talking but was too far away to hear them. At that moment another voice came into my head—Ed choking on his words as I stood on Canal Street, three or four people behind me waiting to use the phone.

Tom Swift was dead. Chris Grady was dead.

Thousands of others were dead.

I grew lightheaded. The earth moved beneath me. I stumbled to a picnic table, sat on top of it, and put my head in my hands. Tears leaked through my fingers. My breath caught. I sobbed. Four arms grabbed and held me. A dog licked my shin.

Samantha's ex-boyfriend—her last serious boyfriend before me—was dead. He'd worked at Cantor Fitzgerald. I remembered her telling me about him. They'd lived together in a railroad apartment with a roommate. One night he cheated on her in their apartment while she was sleeping in the next room. She found him with a strange girl in their roommate's bed the next morning. They still talked sometimes and one day she came to my cubicle looking pissed. She said she'd talked to him and he told her he'd just won the lottery. It wasn't a huge jackpot but it was a nice chunk of change. That's just like him, she said, shaking her head, he's the kind of guy who fucks over his girlfriend and then wins the lottery. His brother also worked at Cantor Fitzgerald and his brother was dead too.

An old friend of mine from Michigan, Justin, who now lived in Astoria but worked in New Jersey, picked me up in the minivan he used for his job.

We drove to Brooklyn. My apartment felt like a museum exhibit of a long-ago time. I'd left one of the kitchen windows open. The air smelled burned. I ran a hand over the table. My fingers came away coated with black grit. I put some clothes in a bag and packed up my laptop. I cleaned the kitchen table with Windex and a sponge.

Back in my room Justin was flipping through my records. He'd put on the Matthew Sweet song "Time Capsule."

—Got everything? he said.

—Yeah. What made you put this on?

—I always liked this song. I haven't heard it in years.

He pulled out the Girls Against Boys album *House of GVSB*.

—That's a great record, I said.

—I don't know about that.

—What do you mean you don't know about that?

—I mean it's not a great record.

—Oh come on. You used to love that record.

—Yeah but that doesn't mean I feel the same way now.

—All right. How do you feel about it now?

—I don't feel anything about it now.

—You don't feel anything?

—No. What's wrong with that?

—Nothing. It's just you played that record a lot.

—So what.

—You played that record constantly and said how great it was. And this was only what—five years ago.

—Tastes change.

—No I know tastes change but it's not like you were lukewarm on this record. It was one of your favorites. You played it every day.

—I don't see your point.

—My point is how could it go from being one of your favorites and playing it every day to totally dismissing it in the span of five years?

—What about you? Your tastes have changed. I bet Nirvana's not your favorite band anymore.

—No but I still like them. I haven't turned my back on them just because I may have moved onto other things.

—When was the last time you listened to *Nevermind*?

—It's been a while. But that doesn't mean I don't think it's a good record.

We walked down Nassau and turned right on Manhattan. I'd never heard the neighborhood so quiet. Even the cars seemed to pass politely in the street. I got some cash at the Citibank. We stopped at Burger King. I snarfed a Double Whopper meal. The atmosphere in Burger King was subdued, only the kids made noise.

We walked east on Manhattan and cut over to Graham. I knocked on Erin's door. She came out smiling and then her eyes filled with tears. Justin went inside. Erin and I stood hugging. Then she pulled away and we just looked at each other. She laughed. She hugged me again.

—Do you remember what you said when you called me?

—No what'd I say?

—You said, I didn't die in that bullshit.

—I didn't die in that bullshit.

—You said it just like that too. Flat. Like a robot.

—Well. It's true.

Remington and his girlfriend and some other people were upstairs. We sat on the roof talking. Erin said she'd seen the whole thing from up here. She'd called Stephen, who now lived in the neighborhood, and he came over and they watched everything happen. She said without Stephen she didn't know what she would've done. She was sure I was dead.

I figured Remington knew about the e-mail I'd sent Baines but I didn't say anything about it and didn't mention Baines. Erin brought him up later after we'd gone back inside. She said Baines had called her to see if I was all right. I said I felt too stupid about what had happened to call him back just now. She said she wasn't sure he wanted me to anyway. I said I guessed that made sense.

Justin, Erin, and I walked around the corner to Stephen's place. We sat watching the news. I used Stephen's phone to check in with my mom.

—Oh good. I've been trying to get a hold of you. Someone from the *Gazette* wants to interview you, she said.

—The *Gazette*?

—Yeah. Hold on, I have his name right here.

She gave me the name and number of the reporter.

I called and told him the story, pausing occasionally as he typed. He said he'd talked to my dad and gotten a DC angle. My mom had given him the number and must have been the one to tell him my dad lived in DC in the first place. We talked for twenty minutes or so. After we hung up I wondered how anyone from the *Kalamazoo Gazette* even knew I worked in the World Trade Center.

Justin and I drove to Clinton Hill. We parked on St. James Place and walked up to an old brownstone. The air smelled of smoke and impending rain. Billie came out. I introduced her to Justin. We went upstairs. Sarah limped into the living room. I hugged her and it felt good because she'd been there and she *knew*.

—Where's Ozzie?

—With my cousin, she said.

—B, you look sunburned, said Billie.

—Do I? I was playing tennis. Maybe I got a little sun.

We sat in the living room and talked about all that we'd seen and experienced the other day. Billie took pictures. Sarah borrowed the camera and took one of me and Billie. I leaned close to her and put my arm around her. She reared back, laughing.

—Oh my god, B, you stink!

—I know. I stopped wearing deodorant.

—You what?

—I stopped wearing deodorant. I'm never wearing it again.

—Uh-huh. And why is that?

—Because. I smell my BO, the reek of my body, and it means I'm alive.

—Can't you be alive and not stink?

—No. Never again. Come here, baby, come smell this.

—You better get your shit away from me, said Sarah.

I huffed at my pit. —God that's beautiful.

She looked at Justin. —Was he always like this?

—I'm afraid so.

Billie mentioned getting back to Queens. Sarah checked her phone and said her man was coming over. No, I said, we have to stay together, don't do this now, don't break us up. Sarah said we had to go—but before we went we were going to pray.

Sarah and Billie stood. Justin and I exchanged a look.

—You too, she said to him.

—That's okay, I said. —You guys go ahead.

—Get up, both of you.

We hesitated a moment. Finally we stood. Billie and Sarah held out their hands. We took them and formed a circle. They closed their eyes and bowed their heads. Justin and I did likewise. We stood in the living room and prayed.

Hard rain driving back. Lightning cut the night sky.

Erin called me in Fair Lawn. I could tell she was crying. Her words tumbled out. *I'm scared here I'm lonely I miss you I barely saw you when you were here.*

—Come to Fair Lawn, I said.

—When?

—Tomorrow. Saturday. Whenever you want.

—You know what the worst part was?

—The worst part of what?

—Watching those buildings, knowing you were there. The worst part was thinking . . . if things were as bad as I thought, as they looked, thinking I just didn't want you to be scared. That's all. I didn't want you to be scared.

—I was scared. I was very scared.

—I know, she said.

My mom called. Another interview request, this time from Channel 3, Kalamazoo's CBS affiliate. They saw my story in the *Gazette* and wanted to do one of their own. I called the station and spoke to a reporter named George. The segment aired multiple times. Stephen called. He was going on the Opie and Anthony radio show and said if I wanted to, if I was up for it, I could call in and talk on the air about my experience. He gave me a number and a time and I called. Samantha forwarded me a message from her brother Jake. Would I mind talking to one of his colleagues at the *Star-Ledger*? Hasna sent an e-mail saying her friend was writing a piece for the *Daily Telegraph* and would I talk to her? The friend was a young British novelist whose book I'd trashed on Amazon without actually reading. After speaking to her I logged onto Amazon and rewrote the review, calling the book elegantly written and pitch-perfect.

Doing the interviews thrilled and vexed me. I started to wish I had a better story to tell. I'd heard about the jumpers but hadn't actually seen them. I'd seen photos and video of office workers fleeing the big cloud covered in dust but wasn't one of them.

A rumor made the rounds about a guy high up in one of the towers who rode the building down as it collapsed and lived. The story was fake but why couldn't it have been real and why couldn't I have been him?

Why couldn't I have been trapped in the rubble—for some short period of time and then removed unharmed? Why couldn't I have been injured—mildly, something that bled a lot but wasn't dangerous, maybe a cut on the arm? Why hadn't I stayed behind to assist helpless individuals—within the narrow time frame before the building collapsed?

My high school creative writing teacher had left a couple of messages. I took one of the phones outside to return her call. Her husband answered. He said Jean would be sorry she missed me. I said that's okay, I could call back. He said she'd really appreciate it and told me when she'd be home.

—Terrible about Brad Hoorn though, isn't it?

—Who?

—That's right, you're a little bit older. You and Brad might not've been at the high school at the same time. How old are you again?

—Twenty-seven.

—So you woulda been—no, Brad was just twenty-three.

—Who's Brad?

—Brad Hoorn. He was a Gull Lake kid. Graduated in ninety-seven. Brad was down there too. He worked in one of the towers.

—What? Which tower?

—Wherever, what's it called, Alger I think it was.

—Alger?

Two Gull Lake kids in the World Trade Center. What were the odds? Gull Lake High School is small. The kids who go there live in small, mostly rural communities.

Two Gull Lake kids in the World Trade Center on the day it's destroyed.

One of them alive. The other one—what?

* * * *

We picked Erin up at the train stop in Radburn and drove back to the place. We stayed up late drinking and then went to bed. I held her but it felt forced and I moved away. I woke sometime in the night, gasping and sweating and holding her tightly.

In the morning we played tennis. I slammed the ball all over the court.

Brad Hoorn.

I called my mom and told her. She already knew. There'd been an article about him in the *Gazette*.

We went to the Empress Diner for lunch. The menu was overwhelming and I couldn't decide. I sat there ravenous while everyone ate. Trish said she wanted to drive around to some yard sales. Erin said that sounded fun. They all split. I walked back to the house and flicked through the channels, searching for news.

Both our stories in the *Kalamazoo Gazette*. Brad Hoorn's family sees mine, my bland tale of survival. I'm a fucking fraud, an exploitative creep.

I wish it was different.

I wish I was gone.

I wish you were the one now telling the tale.

Erin and I lay in bed.

—What's wrong? she asked.

—What do you mean?

—You don't want me near you, I can tell.

—No it's not that. I'm just tired is all.

—I came all the way out here and you hardly even look at me.

—Erin—

—You won't even hug me. It's like you can't stand me being here. And *you* invited me. Come to Fair Lawn, you said.

—I know.

—That's it? You *know*?

—What do you want me to say?

—Anything, Bryan. Anything. You can talk to me.

—Okay. What do you want to talk about?

—Whatever you want. Just don't lay there and act cold, don't . . .

—What?

—I can feel it in your body, you're so distant.

—I'm not—

—You know what you did last night?

—What?

—You grabbed me so hard it woke me up. And you were holding me and it wasn't just a hug it was . . . I don't know. Something else.

—I don't remember that.

—Well it happened.

Silence.

—What, she said, —are you not talking now?

—No I'm talking, I'm just . . .

—What?

—Erin I'm tired. And I just want to fucking go to sleep.

Emergency offices were close to functional. Scuttlebutt placed our group at Harborside Financial Center in Jersey City. There'd been other conference calls. I'd blown them off. Whelan listened in on one. It was disgusting, he said, I should never have called in. No one knew anything, everyone talked in circles. Lois praised the quick thinking of an executive from our floor who'd gotten out of the building, making no mention of the people in her group who'd done likewise. Candy made a crack about her sales binders filling the sky when the plane hit. Binders, said Whelan, people are jumping and she's talking about binders, she wasn't even there and she's talking about binders. Charlotte mentioned an interview she'd done with the *Times*. Look for it, they may or may not quote me, she said. Whelan couldn't take it. He said he'd hung up without a word.

George from Channel 3 called. He said he'd heard from my mom I was planning a trip home. I said that was true. He said she'd told him I was taking the bus in and would be arriving on Tuesday. I confirmed that as well.

—Well we were thinking here at the station—and please feel free to say no, I would completely understand—but we were wondering if you'd mind if we did a story on your homecoming. We'd be there with your parents when you got off the bus.

—We?

—Yes, me and a cameraman. We'd shoot some footage and maybe do a quick interview. Does that sound like something you'd be interested in?

—I don't know.

—Again there's absolutely no pressure. I'll understand completely if, you know, you're not up for it.

—No I'm—I could be up for it.

—You sure?

—Yeah. I guess that'd be okay.

—Great. So you're coming in, what was it your mom said? I have it written down right here. Tuesday the eighteenth?

—Right.

—And you'll be in around noon?

—I'd have to double check but yeah. That sounds right.

—Great. So we'll see you then. Just give a call if anything changes.

After hanging up I dialed my parents' number. My mother answered. I asked why she'd called the news people without my consent.

—I didn't think you'd mind.

—You didn't think I'd mind?

—No. I just made a quick call and said my son's coming home. And that was it.

—Bullshit. The guy had my whole fucking itinerary.

—Who'd you talk to, George?

—Yes. I talked to George.

—Well when I said you were coming in he wanted to know when.

—Of course he wanted to know when! Because you called and told him I was coming! What kind of circular fucking logic is that?

—I don't see why you're upset.

—Of course not. Of course you don't.

—Bryan it'll just take a m—

—Right but mom did it ever occur to you that maybe I don't want to be greeted by news people the moment I step off the bus? Did you ever think maybe I'd just like to see you and Ed?

—I think it'll be good for people in the community to see some good news about this whole thing for a change. Don't you?

—Me? I'm the good news?

—Yeah. You are. You may not realize it now—

—I may not what? I may not realize it?

—I don't know. Do you?

—Don't change the subject.

—I'm not changing the subject. You don't want to do it. Fine. Don't do it. It's no skin off my nose. I just thought—

—I don't care what you thought.

—No?

—No. You should've asked me what *I* thought before calling some fucking news people.

—Maybe I should've. Maybe I should've. But I was a journalist—

—So?

—I was a journalist once. And I know a good story when I see one.

—It's not a fucking story. Mom. It's my life.

—I'm aware of that.

—Are you?

—Yes. I know you think—

—No you don't. You don't know what I think.

—I don't?

—No. You have no idea what I'm thinking.

—All right.

—They knew when I was coming in. You t—

—So don't do it. I just thought—

—I already agreed to it.

—You did?

—Yes.

—Good. You'll see. I think it'll be good for the people in this area to just see a happy ending come out of this whole thing for once.

—Since when do you decide what's good for the people in the area?

—Bryan—

—Don't call anyone else, Mom. Please.

Max sent a mass e-mail encouraging everyone to take time and process the event in their own way. *Write, paint, dance*, he wrote, *there's no one way to heal*. Max and I ended up talking on the phone. He said he'd basically been drunk and high since it happened. He said it was wild when you thought about it—the date of the attack was Nine One One, how crazy was that? He said it was interesting—we were among the few people in our department who were in the building when the plane hit.

—It's like we have this bond now, he said.

* * * *

The night before I left for Michigan, Frank drove in from Long Island and picked me up at my place. Patrick and Mattie were with him. We drove to Forest Hills and found Jenny's building. When I saw her come out my heart did weird things. It was the first time I'd seen her—or anyone in my group—since the attack. She squeezed into the back with Patrick and Mattie. She asked what kind of food we were in the mood for. We discussed it for a minute, settling on Chinese.

Jenny directed us to a sit-down joint she knew. It was empty. The dining room was bright. Two or three waiters hovered, tending instantly to our every need. I ate a huge amount and still felt hungry. I stole long looks at Jenny, hoping for eye contact that affirmed or announced . . . *something*. It never came.

A waiter brought quartered oranges and fortune cookies. We cracked open the cookies and read our fortunes aloud. We sat for a long time nursing waters and talking. Then we paid the bill and left.

Frank pulled up in front Jenny's building. I walked her to the front door.

—Well, she said.

I'm not ready to leave you. I need this night to continue. Give your boyfriend the boot. Invite me in. Come here and kiss me. Open your mouth.

—I just . . . wanted to tell you . . .

My throat clenched. I looked down.

—I'm glad you were with me, I said.

—Hey, she said quietly, —call me anytime.

—All right.

I hugged her. Her embrace was too weak, her words weren't emphatic, her body didn't pulse with electric heat like she *knew*.

Where is the panic? Where are your tears? We cheated death together, exited the inferno alive. We walked through the heart of a blasted city together. Take me in your arms like you mean it. Open your heart to me like you *know*—

I got in the car. Mattie was the only one talking now. She kept saying she felt numb. I looked out the window and cried soundlessly.

—Are you okay, Bryan? said Patrick.

The little lights of the world blipped and streaked.

Galesburg Man

I arrived at the Port Authority early and ate a Double Whopper meal. I stopped at a Verizon kiosk to buy a cellphone. When I came to the portion of the contract asking for work information I told the clerk my office got blown up and he looked at me with wonder and sympathy and I enjoyed it. At Hudson News all the magazine covers showed the towers burning or Two World Trade Center exploding or about to be struck by a shadowy second plane. I flipped through a few and stared at the pictures of people jumping or trapped leaning out of windows on the higher floors. I skimmed the *New Yorker*. What I read enraged me. All those geeks could do in the face of this was fashion their impotent similes. Now they were the ones with their faces pressed to the glass. I bought a copy of *Harry Potter and the Prisoner of Azkaban* and walked out. A short time later I boarded my bus. It left the station and moved slowly into New Jersey. Somewhere in Pennsylvania we stopped at a McDonald's. I stood in the parking lot looking out at the little town. Already it seemed I was light years from New York. Several hours later I fell asleep picturing my death: it's late at night, the driver's exhausted, he falls asleep, crashes through a guardrail, flies down a ravine, we all die instantly. We pulled into Cleveland around two a.m. I was sitting on a bench in the bus station when a little dot of white light formed in my field of vision, as if I'd just seen a camera flash. I bought a Coke and slammed it. Caffeine didn't help. The white dot bloomed. I lost focus. Strange shapes resembling little gears appeared and pulsed with multicolored light. I grew nauseous and walked outside. I boarded my next bus three-quarters blind. Half an hour later my vision returned, followed by an unspeakable throb in my head. The pain intensified. I couldn't sleep. I went to the bathroom and wiped my neck with a moist towelette. In Detroit I sat on a bench outside the bus station staring at a casino in the distance. Dawn was breaking. I boarded another bus. We hit I-94 and stopped in Ann Arbor. Albion. Battle Creek. The fast food and gas station signs said GOD BLESS USA and NEVER FORGET and BLESS OUR HEROES and STRONGER THEN EVER and UNITED WE STAND. I hadn't eaten in almost twenty-four hours. The migraine had left me trembling and spent. I could almost have been hallucinating this familiar landscape, the feeling of home. Let me die in Michigan. Not in some fucking city. No need to bury or burn me. Throw me in the swamp or the woods. Let the animals eat me. I want to die here. I don't want to go back. We passed the Galesburg exit and the Thirty-fifth Street exit and got off on the Kalamazoo business loop. There was almost no one on the bus now, just me and four or five others. We turned left on Michigan Avenue. The bus station was a mile or so down on the right. There was a gathering under the awning where the buses park. My mom and Ed. A man in a suit holding a News 3 microphone, a man with a News 3 camera standing next to him. A guy with a spiral notebook, a guy with a regular camera. A guy wearing a shirt and tie holding what looked like a pizza box. Jean, my high school creative writing teacher, and her husband.

A man behind me noticed the news crew. —They must be waitin on some of them rescue workers comin back from New York, he said.

I wanted to correct him. I wanted to say no, actually they're waiting for me. And then I wanted to tell him why and I wanted him to give me *that look*. I went to the bathroom and wiped my hands with a moist towelette. The bus lurched to a stop. The air brakes hissed. I walked to the front of the bus, down the steps, and out the door. My parents embraced me. The cameraman filmed us. The guy with the regular camera snapped pictures. Ed's arms were around me holding my mom between us.

—This is better than bein a Vietnam hero, he said.

I blinked away tears.

Jean gave me a small bouquet with an American flag sticking out of it.

The man holding the pizza box was a representative from my local congressman's office. I was told that the box held an American flag and the text of a speech the congressman had given. The lackey handed me the box and split.

The man with the notebook was the *Gazette* reporter I'd talked to previously. He asked me some questions for a follow-up story to be published the next day.

I spoke with George, from Channel 3. I said I was happy to be back but it was bittersweet. I said my thoughts were with the families of those still missing. I mentioned Tom Swift and Brad Hoorn.

We were getting ready to leave when George came over. They'd reviewed some of the footage. There was a problem with the audio. The idling buses had drowned us out.

—Would you mind if we came out to your house and talked to you there?

—All right, I said.

My mom gave him directions.

The story ran on the five, five-thirty and six o'clock broadcasts, with slight variations in length and editing each time. There's me stepping off the bus into the arms of my parents. There's me waving from the passenger seat of Ed's truck as we circle the parking lot and drive off. There's me sitting in a chair in the backyard on a bright sunny day, looking pale and exhausted, explaining how it feels to be home. There's my mom talking about where she was when she first heard a plane had crashed into the World Trade Center—coming out of the locker room at the Sherman Lake Y— and what it was like to finally get my call. There's George in the studio chatting with the anchor team about our visit, saying Bryan has a good head on his shoulders, I think he's gonna come out of this okay. Aside from the bus station footage there was nothing from Ed. George had asked for an interview at the house but Ed said no and disappeared.

It all made me cringe, especially the bus station embrace. I remembered tearing up. I'd been aware of the camera. Had I been playing to it? Was I truly overwhelmed? Were my emotions at that moment even real?

I opened the box with the flag and read the congressman's speech. It had been delivered on the House floor on the night of September 12.

> . . . This has been a long day for America, as we come to grip with this attack and the values we hold so dear. I spoke earlier this afternoon with a family from my district whose son, Brad, worked on the ninety-third floor. Their news was no news. No word. No good. And as we struggle with our grief and pray for those families, we are reminded that this is a country that stands for freedom and justice. And, yes, we will prevail. We stand here tonight united behind our nation's efforts to seek swift justice. We *will* find *all the people* who orchestrated and participated in this evil web. I have no doubt. These mass murderers wherever they are will be identified, and yes, justice will be served . . .

* * * *

After my parents went to bed I went to the basement, sat at my mom's computer, and wrote everything I could remember about last Tuesday. I wrote without pausing to fuss over language or fix things. Now and then I closed my eyes, trying to remember certain details more clearly. I filled five single-spaced pages with a single unbroken paragraph. I printed the pages and brought them upstairs. I lay in bed with the fan on and soon was asleep. An explosion jolted me awake. I looked around in a panic, unsure of where I was. Rain poured down. Lightning flashed. Thunder boomed. I lay back, still terrified, and listened to the storm. Something was working toward me. I sensed my life would end suddenly, violently, prematurely. I knew now that life had no pattern or meaning. I knew now that I would never be safe.

Greg and his friend Popper drove in from Chicago in a rented car. I met them at Greg's parents' house off Oakland Drive. Greg and Popper had visited me in New York the week before it happened. On Friday afternoon they'd come up to the office. I'd shown them around. We sat now in the small apartment behind the garage. Greg took a hit of his cigarette and blew smoke.

—Bryan I have to tell you. When I called your parents and your stepdad told me you were all right I started crying with him still on the phone.

—You did? What a pussy.

—Look, said Popper. —I still have this, what do you call it, this little thing here.

He showed me his temporary ID card. *Lance Popper. 2 WTC. Visitor. 09/07/01.*

We drove to Vine Street and parked. We walked around the old neighborhood. Greg and I riffed on former times.

Remember when we thought the hippies next door were stealing our water to irrigate their pot plants and you crawled into their yard and slashed their hose with a knife and left the knife sticking through the hose into the ground?

Remember when the kid with the head injury was visiting upstairs and all he ate was eggs, he kept making eggs, and one night he put a tape in and rapped over "Wind Beneath My Wings" and he kept apologizing, saying he knew the beats were shitty but check out his rhymes?

We went to Martini's and wolfed calzones. We walked north on Westnedge to Bronson Park. We sat at a picnic table and talked for a while. Then we crossed Rose Street and headed over to what had once been the downtown walking mall, the first open-air mall in the country, it was said. The Kalamazoo Mall had fallen on years of hard times. All the shopping action had moved to the strip malls and chain stores in Portage. They'd dug up the walking mall the summer I left. They put a road in hoping to draw people back downtown. New stores and restaurants had opened up. We walked along scoping the supposedly revitalized scene.

On Michigan Avenue we entered the parking structure across from the Radisson. We walked to the top and looked out at the city. I leaned over the edge and looked down at the sidewalk, feeling a strange itch, a strong urge to jump.

At Harvey's people stared at me with undisguised amazement. One guy stood with his mouth open, shaking his head. Fuck, he kept saying, fuck, what was it like being there for the start of World War Three?

I walked upstairs and out to the deck. I ran into Courtney, one of my former obsessive crushes. In college we'd had a class together, Film Communication. I spent that semester in agony, pondering how I could make her mine. I typed up a crush letter and sent it in the mail. A year later I asked her out. She said yes but called a few days later to cancel. Her great aunt had died and she had to go to the funeral, she said. She'd call back soon to reschedule. But she never called back and our date never happened. All my friends knew her as my Film Class Crush.

—How long you in town for? she asked.

—About a week.

—Read about you in the paper. Saw you on TV.

—Yeah well.

I looked out at Burdick Street.

—You know the weird thing about that?

—Lotta things, I imagine.

—Yeah but the really weird part? Hearing myself described as *man*. Galesburg man tells of escape from trade center.

—Why's that weird?

—*Man*? That doesn't seem right. I don't feel like a man.

—No? What should they have said then?

—*Guy* sounds better. Galesburg guy flees trade center. Or dude. That sounds about right. Galesburg dude almost dies.

I felt people's eyes on me as I walked through the bar. Greg and Popper were sitting at a booth outside. I walked out and sat next to Popper. A girl came over and started talking to Greg. I remembered seeing her at all-ages shows in the early nineties. She was talking nonstop, saying she lived in New York.

—I mean, you know, I used to, she said.

—Really? I said. —I live there now.

—Bryan worked in the World Trade Center, said Greg.

—Oh my god. Really? I worked there too.

—Where di—

—At the Gap in the mall. Can you fucking believe it? It is so fucked up. I mean seriously. It's like. I was there every day. Every day. I mean literally. Fuck.

She paused to light a cigarette.

—But you live here now?

She nodded and exhaled.

—I moved back last year.

—How long were you in the city?

—Six months. But I love it. I'm just. I'm like. I can't fucking believe it. It's like. You know? I used to go there like. Every day.

She went on and on about how fucked up it was that she used to work in the Gap in the World Trade Center. She couldn't get her mind around it, it really was too much.

I borrowed a neighbor's bike and rode up G Avenue. I turned right on Thirty-sixth Street and followed it down and over to Thirty-fifth Street. I rode past trees and cornfields. I heard wind in the trees and the sound of my breath and the tires on the road. The sky was a cloudless blue. I breathed the clean air. I rode down to Three Lakes and stopped for a while. I looked across the water at the trees on the other side of the lake. I listened to the water lapping on the small sandy shore. Then I got on the bike and rode home.

After the drama of my homecoming and the excitement of the interviews—the local ABC affiliate had contacted me and come to the house too—things were pretty much the same. Ed sat in his chair flipping through the channels, stopping when he came to a western or a fishing show or the weather. Now and then he'd get up and go look for something to do in the basement or the yard. He and my mom went on their evening walks. They drank coffee on the back porch after dinner and watched TV at night. My mom came home from Blockbuster with two movies she thought would speak to me in my current state of mind: *The Day of the Jackal*, about a plot to assassinate Charles de Gaulle, and *Fearless*, starring Jeff Bridges as a stunned plane-crash survivor who be-friends fellow survivor Rosie Perez.

One afternoon I drove to the Crossroads Mall. I hadn't packed enough clothes and needed to buy socks. I could've done this at Meijer's, a short drive away, but I had an ulterior motive for going all the way out to the mall. I wanted to be recognized. I wanted to run into someone who would give me *that look*. It didn't take long. On the upper level by Frederick's of Hollywood I heard my name and stopped. An older woman with glasses was walk-ing toward me, a man I presumed to be her husband following a few steps behind. She introduced herself and mentioned a vague connection we had, something involving a high school acquaintance of mine. She told me she'd seen me on the news and that she was happy I'd made it out alive. I thanked her and moved on.

I drove to a neighboring complex of strip malls and entered Barnes & Noble. I lingered at the front of the store flipping through *The Corrections*. Two weeks earlier I'd read a profile of Jonathan Franzen in the *New York Times Magazine* in which he came off as an insufferable prick. He bragged about how ambi-tious he was, said he wrote wearing earplugs and a blindfold, challenged the writer to guess how many manuscript pages he'd thrown away in the creation of his masterpiece. Still, *The Corrections* was the hot book of the moment and I was eager to keep up. I gave up waiting for someone to see me and brought the book to the check-out line. As I was waiting I heard my name.

It was a girl I went to high school with. She was two years be-hind me. She'd dated a friend of mine who lived in a mansion on Gull Lake. I remember she never seemed to know what to say to me. I was just this weird guy who was always hanging around. She looked at me now with wonder and sympathy.

—I heard you were in the World Trade Center, she said.

* * * *

On my last night in town I met my film class crush at her loft in the 666 building. We walked to Kraftbrau and drank a few pints. We stood out on the deck in the cooling night. A train passed on the railroad tracks several feet from us. One of the men on the train looked at us and held up a hand.

Back at her pad we sat looking at old photos. Courtney kept leaning over me reaching for pictures to show me. It gave me a surge of desire each time.

It was one in the morning. We went into the living room. I sat in a chair in the corner. Courtney stood over me with her camera and snapped a picture. I got up and said it was time to shove off.

—I'll walk you down, she said.

Halfway down the stairs I turned and asked if I could kiss her. She closed her eyes, smiled, said yes. We kissed in the stairwell leaning against the wall. Her breath tasted faintly of smoke. I touched her face and hair and ran my hands over her breasts. She kissed my neck. I kissed her cheek and her closed eyes. I remembered in film class thinking she had cool sleepy eyes and how I dreamed of kissing her as we sat next to each other watching *The 400 Blows*.

Why are you doing this now? Is it because of what I've been through? Do you just want to be close to it like everyone else?

At the bottom of the stairs we kissed some more.

—Have a safe trip back, she said.

I looked through the glass doors. My mom's Nissan Sentra was parked across the street next to the railroad tracks. It seemed an incredible distance away.

—Will you watch and make sure I get to the car okay?

Courtney laughed. —Sure, she said.

I opened the door and walked out. My footsteps seemed to be the only sound in the city. The night felt like it would swallow me whole and leave no trace. Halfway to the car I turned around to make sure she was still there.

It was almost three when I got back to Galesburg. Six hours later Paul and Trish pulled in. They were leaving soon for another long Youth Stream tour and had driven Barney to Petoskey to stay with Paul's mom. My mom and Ed walked me out to the driveway. I said goodbye to them and got in the car. We drove straight through to Fair Lawn. The next day, Sunday, I took the train back to New York.

Strange Communication from a Distant Galaxy

Charles, Bryan

From: adminfeedback@morganstanley.com
Sent: Thursday, September 13, 2001 12:36 PM
To: Undisclosed Recipients
Cc: adminfeedback@morganstanley.com
Subject: Cancellation Notice: IM: 360 PE: Feedbacking Your Peers (WTC)

Please be advised that the following course has been CAN-CELLED:

We apologize for the inconvenience.

IM: 360 PE: Feedbacking Your Peers (WTC)

Start Date: Sep-11-2001 End Date: Sep-11-2001

Start Time: 1:30 PM End Time: 3:30 PM

Location: 2WTC 72nd Floor Boardroom (2 World Trade Center, Floor: 72ND)

Important: You will NOT be automatically re-enrolled in this course. Please review course availability and re-register at your convenience.

Thank You.

The BIF

The Business Interruption Facility was a large room filled with rows of tables with old computer monitors on them. There were little American flags on sticks taped to the side of each monitor. Two hundred or so people from various departments sat elbow to elbow at the tables in third-hand office chairs or folding chairs. It was loud and hot. In the back was a room with more tables and coolers. The tables were covered with baskets of Pop-Tarts, Nutter Butters, Oreos, Hershey bars, Fritos, Rice Krispie Treats, chocolate balls, chocolate drops, SunChips, pretzels, potato chips, Lorna Doones, Famous Amos, snack-size peanuts, Quaker Oat bars, Nutri-Grain bars, Sunflower Nutty Nuggets, shiny waxed green apples, bunches of spotted bananas. The coolers were stocked with water and juice and hundreds of cans of Pepsi and Coke. There were dispensers of regular and decaf coffee, baskets of sugar-free sweeteners and nondairy creamers. Every day around noon a free lunch was wheeled in. A line formed along the far wall of the BIF. People entered the food room on one side and came out the other side holding paper plates piled high with pepper steak and curly fries or eggplant parmesan or cheese tortellini or hamburgers or veggie burgers or General Tso's chicken or tuna salad sandwiches. In the front of the room were two tables for eating or lounging but those filled up quickly so lunch was typically eaten at your work station, where you were packed so tightly you could hear the people around you biting, chewing, sipping, swallowing, burping under their breath. There were few food options outside the Harborside complex so if you wanted to eat elsewhere you could take a prepaid meal card and eat at a food court called the Harborside Club that had grill, sandwich, and pasta stations. If you wanted to step out for some air you could walk to the waterfront, stand at the rail, and look over at the smoke billowing out of the hole directly across the river.

There weren't enough seats for our group in the BIF. A rotating schedule was established where people worked in the BIF some days and offsite other days. My offsite location was on Spring Street, in the offices of the design firm that produced our materials. At either location I did very little.

In the BIF I ate constantly and fried my mind on the Internet. Billie and Sarah were seated on another part of the floor that had actual offices and cubicles. I spent a lot of time over there talking to them.

There were dozens of new women around, displaced workers from other groups and other floors. I ran sex fantasies nonstop. I wanted to fuck constantly. I would fixate on new women daily, imagine fucking them in some hidden nook somewhere — or better yet in the food room, business-casual clothes sweaty, torn half off, bare asses crunching bags of cookies and chips.

On Spring Street I read the Internet and wrote in my journal. Often I would leave the office and take long walks. One day I went up to St. Mark's Bookshop and saw that Baines's story had come out in the *Paris Review*. I read the first couple pages and put it back on the shelf.

I stopped shaving, figured I would try to grow my first beard.

* * * *

Frank, Patrick, and I left work early and took a ferry across the river. We made our way without speaking up to the site. The sidewalks were jammed with tourists taking pictures. Certain streets were blocked off. It was difficult to get around. The air had an acrid burning-chemical smell. Black smoke rose from the pile. The charred, broken shell of Five World Trade Center was visible. We stood looking for a while. None of us spoke. Then we started to make our way south. On Broadway and Dey Street a woman stood holding a tray of cookies in front of a new establishment called Cookie Island. A banner over the sign said GRAND OPENING. The woman smiled helplessly as we approached.

—Free sample? she said.

—Sure.

We each took a cookie and ate.

Shortly before the attack, as a result of Bush's massive tax overhaul, I'd received my three hundred dollar rebate check from the government. I brought the check to work and put it in a drawer. Along with a folder of old manuscripts it was the only thing of any value in my desk. I'd been conflicted about the check. In a weird way I saw it as a slap in the face. Certainly three hundred dollars was nothing to sneeze at. But I knew the real beneficiaries of the tax cuts were the wealthy and to those most in need three hundred dollars would likely be negligible. In a minor act of protest—my first—I'd planned on donating the money to charity rather than using it for its stated purpose, shopping. I'd been trying to decide which charity when the building was destroyed.

Now I felt differently. Now I wanted my money.

Sitting in the BIF I dialed a general information number for the IRS. I was transferred around till I got the right department. I explained the situation, thinking the words World Trade Center would open all doors. I was told the period for cutting new checks had passed.

—Right but surely you understand. This is sort of an usual situation.

—I understand that, sir. But—

—I mean I'm not making this up here. This isn't some scam.

—Sir I'm not sug—

—Check your records, your logs or whatever. I haven't cashed it or anything. The check doesn't exist anymore.

—Sir if you had—

—What? If I had what? Called a month ago, before the check was destroyed?

—There was a window in which we were cutting substitute checks.

—Yes?

—And I'm afraid there's not—there's just nothing we can do at this point. Now what I *can* do is put you in touch with a tax-payer advocate who c—

—A what?

—A taxpayer advocate.

—Okay. What's that?

—A taxpayer advocate is someone who'll work with you t—

—You know what? No. I don't wanna talk to any taxpayer advocate. I just want my three hundred fucking dollars.

—Sir please—

—Do you understand what I'm telling you here? My check was in the World Trade Center. Do you know what that means? Do you watch the news?

I sensed watchers, listeners. Charlotte sat an inch from me, staring at her monitor. I raised my voice and continued.

—I didn't even *want* that check. Did you know that? I mean come on, three hundred dollars? Do you have any idea what three hundred dollars even buys these days?

—Sir I'm tr—

—Not a whole lot. And I'll tell you another thing. I didn't vote for George Bush and I didn't want his fucking tax cuts. But what I want you to do now is click the little box on your computer that says you'll send me a new check. My other check blew up. And I need a new one.

Silence.

—Sir I'm truly sorry. I am. But there's noth—

I slammed the phone down. Charlotte's Coke splashed on her keyboard. She cursed me. I sat there shaking. I got up and left.

Saturday night I ordered Thai food and watched a Yankees–Devil Rays game on TV. It was a boring game and the Devil Rays won. After that I called Billie. We talked for a while and then I called Sarah. I knew she'd bought a used car in Atlanta and had driven it back to New York. I told her I was lonely and begged her to come pick me up. Sarah said she was strapped and made me promise to pay her gas money. An hour later she called from the street. Ozzie was in the passenger seat, sleeping through Alicia Keys. I got in back. We drove to Sarah's place. She put Ozzie to sleep in her bed. We lay on the couch in the living room. We held each other and talked. It was the first time we'd ever been this close.

The lights were out. The TV was on at a low volume, filling the room with its soothing glow. I was attracted to Sarah but there was something else tied up in it now too. The thing I'd been looking for in Jenny's eyes at the Chinese restaurant—a mix of ecstasy, horror, fear, the awareness of the frailty and absurdity of life—was here in this room. We lay there talking till after midnight. It was comforting just to lie in her arms.

She slept in her bed with Ozzie. I slept on Ozzie's twin bed in his closet-size room. I made Sarah dig out a fan so I could hear the white noise.

Ozzie woke me early the next morning by grabbing my hand and slapping me five. We watched Looney Tunes together till Sarah got up.

On the drive back to my place Ozzie put in a Jadakiss CD and cranked it. "We Gonna Make It" filled the car. Listening to that song on the BQE, Brooklyn speeding past me, I felt large and powerful, like the three of us—and maybe only the three of us—were safe and would be all right somehow. *Fuck the frail shit.*

Later that day Erin rode her bike over. I hadn't seen her since the weekend at Paul and Trish's, though we'd talked on the phone a few times. We sat in my room talking. I got up and went to the bathroom. When I came back she was sitting at my desk. I lay on the bed. There was a moment of silence. Erin turned to me.

—So what'd you say you did last night?

—Last night? Nothing. Ordered Amarin. Watched the Yankees.

—Who's Sarah?

—What?

She looked away. —I'm such an idiot, she said.

—What are you talking about?

—I read your journal.

—You w—

—Just now. When you were in the bathroom. I read it.

It was there on the desk next to her elbow.

—You read my journal?

—I didn't mean to. I saw some papers sticking out of it and opened it for a second. I saw the date. You wrote you were lying around with a girl named Sarah.

—Sarah's my coworker. I work with her.

—Right. Just like you *worked* with Samantha.

—Erin—

—I thought it was one of your stories. You always show me your stories. And I went to look at it and it just happened.

—Erin listen to me—

—What? You've done it. You read Elise Pratt's journal. Remember? You used to tell me about it and laugh.

I lay back and stared straight ahead.

—Maybe you should leave.

—What? It was an accident, Bryan. Bryan. Look at me.

I looked at her and didn't say anything.

—You are so cruel to me. How can you be so cruel to me, Bryan?

—I don't know.

—God the way you're looking at me right now. If you could see your face. If you could hear your voice the way I hear it. What's the matter with you?

I turned away from her. She sat in the chair and cried. I lay there looking at my stereo. After a few minutes she stood and walked out of the room and out of the apartment. I could hear her crying in the hallway and all the way down the stairs. The window was open. I heard her unlock her bike and pedal away.

I came out of the PATH station and walked toward Harborside. Across from Harborside at another big complex hundreds of people were standing on the sidewalk and in the street. Office workers continued to file out of the building. There were several cop cars and an ambulance out front.

—What the hell happened? I asked a guy next to me.

—Bomb scare, he said.

I continued on to the BIF, where I sat with Whelan and some others. Soon we all left. We rode in a convoy of vans through Jersey City and arrived at a church. The pews filled in. Tom Swift's memorial service began. I stared at a laminated photo that had been given out with the programs. It had been taken the day Tom got his MBA. He wore a cap and gown and was smiling. Some of Tom's friends spoke and then his brother came up. His brother resembled him and as he was speaking I started to cry.

—I love you, Tommy, he said, —forever and ever and ever.

I began to resent the firefighters-and-cops-as-heroes narrative being spun by the mayor, the media, and to a certain extent the firefighters and cops themselves. Initially I'd been swept up in it too. I referred to rescue workers as heroes in several interviews. I praised the steady hand of Giuliani, whom I'd long considered a creep. As the days wore on—as people continued to applaud and salute passing fire trucks, to speak and write with reverence of the unparalleled bravery and quick thinking of the firemen they claimed had saved countless lives—it began to eat away at me. I'd seen the photos of firemen going up the stairwell as everyone else went down. But I'd personally seen no rescue workers or security people till I was down on the mezzanine. That didn't mean they weren't there. Obviously they were and several hundred of them had died. I didn't discount that. But of the casualties, many hundreds more—into the thousands, no one knew the precise number—were workaday employees of all varieties doing unglamorous jobs. Weren't their lives in a sense heroic? Didn't they deserve elaborate funerals with heads of state in attendance and dramatic bagpipe salutes? Didn't they deserve the applause of the masses? Yes, the firemen had gone against human instinct and entered a burning building. But thousands of people were already inside, fighting fear and chaos and the unknown. It's not like each one of us was carried to safety on the back of a cool-headed fireman. No, the only official word we got was that things were under control and to go sit back down. Wasn't there anything heroic about confused and scared-shitless office workers keeping it together—*banding* together—enough to buck the odds and make it out alive?

* * * *

The terrible days passed. I waited for the other shoe to drop. Every time the subway or PATH train slowed to a halt in the tunnel a deep sense of unease would permeate the train car. I panicked if I didn't hear an announcement immediately. When the announcement came I'd study the conductor's voice for a sign that it wasn't just train traffic that delayed us, that in fact something was terribly wrong. The feeling was especially acute if we were under one of the rivers.

I braced myself daily for further explosions. My nerves were constantly crackling and hot. I started tuning in to *Smallville* weekly. I scoffed at the very notion of Superman and ran make-out fantasies starring the babe who played Lana.

Other times I'd sit on the couch and just stare.

Ginny stopped by and asked if we could talk for a second. We walked into an office furnished only with two chairs. She closed the door and we sat.

—How are you doing? she asked.

—All right. How are you?

—Good days and bad.

—It's strange that your wedding was there right before it happened. You and Ward must have been some of the last people to get married there.

—Yeah. I've thought about that.

—I didn't want to go down there on a weekend. A Sunday. I thought why couldn't she have picked somewhere else to get married.

Ginny smiled.

—You and Frank both.

—Now I'm glad it was there. I'm glad I went.

—I am too.

She looked at her hands.

—I don't want to pry, she said.

—All right.

—It's just, you don't seem like you're taking things well.

—Well. It's a hard situation. The BIF's an uncomfortable place.

—I don't mean just the BIF.

—I know what you mean.

—Have you thought about talking to someone?

—You mean like a therapist?

—Or . . . yeah. A therapist.

—Have I thought about it? Sure.

—They have counselors here, onsite. You can go anytime.

—I've heard that.

—Dana and I were talking about going. Why don't you come with us.

—I don't know. I don't think so.

—You sure? It might be good to talk to someone.

—I know. It might be. I'm just . . .

—Yeah?

I looked at her and shrugged.

—All right. Do me a favor though?

—Sure.

—Just think about it at least.

—All right.

—You mean it?

—Yes. I'll think about it.

—You know Lois came up to me and mentioned your shoes.

—My shoes?

—She said why is Bryan wearing tennis shoes?

I glanced at my feet. I was wearing gray Nikes with a blue swoosh, the ones I'd bought at the Mall of America. My work shoes had been under my desk. I hadn't gotten around to buying a new pair.

—I like these shoes. They're my lucky shoes. They got me down seventy flights.

—Lois wants you to wear work shoes.

—Does she? What about the executives she's so happy survived. Does she approve of their footwear?

—Probably, said Ginny.

—I'm sorry. I don't want to put you in a weird position.

—It's okay. Just think about what I said.

—I will.

Morgan Stanley was launching the Charitable Gift Program. Max's group had written the materials. The hook was that many investors had achieved stupendous wealth in the last decade and surely were now looking for ways to give back. The Charitable Gift Program offered potential do-gooders easy, one-stop philanthropy—as well as a host of attractive tax breaks. It was to be the feature story in the next issue of *Fund Update Quarterly*. I was told the surge of donations in the wake of the attack would make a nice tie-in. At my work station in the BIF I wrote:

> In the days after September 11, the families of the victims of the attacks on New York and Washington DC received a tremendous outpouring of emotional and financial support. Now, as we move into 2002, our nation is stronger than ever and Americans realize that giving is a year-round activity. We must never forget the events of that tragic day. Embracing the humanity it brought out of us by continuing to give all that we can is a good start.

Writing these words sickened me. It also brought me a measure of relief. I saw what I would have to do now to try to stay sane.

* * * *

The novel would be called *Stay Cool Forever*. It would begin the day Vim Sweeney graduated high school and would follow him through the summer. In the early pages he would quit his dishwashing job and have adventures. I didn't know what those adventures would be. I only knew he'd fall in love with a girl who was dating the drummer in his band and meet an older woman to whom he might or might not lose his virginity. I had enough material for the first thirty or forty pages. What I needed now was time. I needed to get away from the BIF. I needed to see who and what I could be without this job that was tearing me to fucking pieces. I needed to write this book. I had almost died. I would have died doing something I hated in a place I didn't want to be. Giuliani had said somewhere that innocent people were in the World Trade Center nobly pursuing their dreams. But I'm no innocent and I wasn't pursuing my dream there, I was watching it die. I knew if I didn't quit my job and try to write this novel it would only get worse. I would hate myself. I already hated myself. I would hate myself more. Very few people end up doing what they want with their lives. I'd been deferring the day that I would try for something more and then a plane hit my building and I had almost died.

I thought of dying constantly. I lay in bed at night and could feel the floor give way beneath me, saw the ceiling cave as the building collapsed. I dreamed my body was a plane flying over the harbor headed straight for the World Trade Center. I dreamed I was inside the World Trade Center and knew what was going to happen and exactly when the planes would hit. Then they hit and I knew how much time we had to get out and watched the minutes tick down on a huge digital clock. I imagined being trapped in a burning conference room with nowhere to go and no way to get out except ahead through the shattered windows. What would I have done? Would I have jumped? I imagined sitting at my desk scrolling through two dozen meaningless e-mails and having a plane crash into me, vaporizing me instantly. I imagined shooting myself, hanging myself, slashing my wrists, overdosing on pills, throwing myself onto the subway tracks as a train entered the station. I didn't want to die, I was terrified of dying, yet I thought of killing myself daily and at times almost wanted to do it. I imagined being in the stairwell when the building collapsed. What would I have felt? What would come next? Sarah told me I'd felt cold when the plane hit because I had no relationship with god. She said if I believed in him I would have felt something different at that moment, I wouldn't have felt cold. Billie agreed with her and urged me to read a book called *Conversations with God*. She said it would help me. I told her I'd think about it. I wanted to say no, don't bother because don't you see there is no fucking god. Think of someone's mother or father or son or daughter sitting on a plane crashing into a building or in a field in Pennsylvania and then tell me there's a god. Think of someone's mother or father or son or daughter burning in a conference room or falling a hundred stories to their death in their work clothes or crushed under two hundred and twenty stories of rubble and then tell me there's a god. Tell me there's a benevolent figure called Jesus who will rise again and walk the earth. Tell me again how he'll save us.

Hasna walked into the apartment and gave me a hug. It was the first time I'd seen her since July of 2000.
  —You're a good hugger, I said.
  —I see you have a beard now.
  —It's a new thing. I never tried growing one before.
  —It suits you.
  —You think so? I'm not so sure.

—I think it looks good.

I laughed. —You're the only one.

We sat on the floor of my room listening to records. All her skin was covered except her face and her hands. I watched her mouth as she talked. I leaned over and kissed her. She was a good kisser and we moved up to the bed. We kissed and I pulled back and looked at her and tried to imagine her hair and what she'd look like without her scarf. I kissed her again.

I wanted to go further. I wanted to see everything. I wanted to remove her scarf, her hooded sweatshirt, her shirt. I wanted to kiss her breasts and stomach and arms. I pressed hard against her. My beard brushed her face. She put her tongue in my mouth. I felt her breath on my lips. I looked at her hands and into her eyes and at her mouth. I kissed her again. I came in my pants. I kissed her some more and then we stopped and just lay just there. I felt dizzy. I moved down on the bed and put my head on her shoulder. I didn't tell her what had happened.

Soon I got up, went to the bathroom, and changed.

My mom would call and ask how I was doing. I told her the truth: that I was so depressed I barely had the energy to walk up the stairs to my place.

—Hmm. Do you want me to come out there and cheer you up? she asked.

—No, I said. —Please.

She came anyway.

The night she flew in we went to an Italian restaurant in Williamsburg. We split a bottle of wine and tempers flared. I had sent her a letter telling her I was thinking of quitting my job. She told me that was a bad idea. She said the best thing for me now would be to move on. I said that was easier said than done. I said the whole experience had fucked me up and didn't she understand I'd just been bombed by terrorists?

She shot forward in her seat and jabbed a finger at me.

—Hey! I lived with a terrorist. Okay?

She meant her father, who by all accounts could be an abusive brute. I'd been hearing the stories my whole life, from my mom and her brothers and sisters. I'd seen it myself as a child on those long-ago drunken Thanksgivings.

—This is what you came here to tell me? I open up to you and try and tell you how I feel and this is what you say to me? That you lived with a terrorist?

It was almost worse when I flew home for Christmas.

Ed picked me up from the airport. Five minutes after we walked through the door my mom mentioned casually, almost as an aside, that the *Gazette* reporter had called for me earlier. He was writing a series of holiday-update stories. He wanted to talk to me and wondered if by chance I was home. My mom had said yes, I was due in today. She told him I'd call him back at three. We had another long argument about her setting up interviews with the press. The more I pushed for an apology the more she insisted she'd done the right thing.

—This is your place in history, she said.

—My *what?*

—That day, after we finally got your call, I was watching all those people talking on TV and I just thought—my *son* was there. Good god. And it just struck me, I mean how *huge* this all is. And I picked up the phone and called the *Gazette*. The minute they heard me say my son was in that building they had me talking to a reporter.

—Great. So now every two months Brad Hoorn's family opens up the paper and they see my fucking face and another goddamn story about how I lived.

—I know you feel bad about that.

—*Bad?* It's not . . . I don't . . .

I didn't have the strength for this. I'd gotten up before dawn to catch my flight. I chewed Xanax like Tic Tacs. It didn't help. The whole time in the air I was certain the plane would crash somehow and that today was my last day alive.

—Why can't you just say you're sorry? I said.

—Because. I think—or *hope*—that in time you'll agree with me.

—About what?

—I really do feel this is your place in history.

—What bullshit, I said.

I called the reporter at three anyway. I knew that I would even as I chastised my mother. She may have taken it a step further than I would have liked. She may have acted rashly and without my permission. But I was more pleased with her media overtures than I admitted. Seeing my name in print was a gas. For years I'd been writing stories and sending them into the world. No one would publish them. No one cared. Now everyone wanted to hear the story I had to tell.

The reporter asked what things had been like for me recently. I told him there'd been a big change since the last time we talked.

Several weeks earlier, just after my mom left New York, I approached Ginny in the BIF and asked to speak with her. We returned to the same empty office where she'd suggested I see a therapist. I told her I couldn't do this job anymore. She said she knew and that she understood. I told her I couldn't do this job anymore and that I wanted to write a novel and I just had to see. She said she thought I was brave. I said I didn't know about that. Ginny convinced me to stay till January so I could at least get my bonus. So I stayed for two more months—endured the BIF for two more months—and as it turned out my bonus was next to nothing. Lois revealed the paltry figure and reminded me we were in the midst of hard times. I said nothing. I didn't care. Lois couldn't touch me now. None of them could touch me now. Nothing and no one could touch me but I was not free.

My last day passed with little fanfare. I was given a card with some cash in it, I don't remember how much. By early afternoon I'd been locked out of the system. I sat waiting for the day to end. I said goodbye to some people but there was no after-work drinks gathering. I left the BIF and went home alone.

The following Monday the clock radio alarm went off at seven. I made coffee and drank it in the living room as I read. I finished the coffee and sat there a while. I walked to the kitchen and rinsed out my cup. I went to the back room and turned on my computer. I opened the document called *Stay Cool Forever*. I stared at the screen and then started to type.

Acknowledgments

Thanks to Thomas Beller, Brooklyn Writers Space, Dianne Charles, Erin Dwight, Fran Dwight, Ryan Gage, the *Kalamazoo Gazette*, the Kalamazoo Public Library, Stephen Lynch, the MacDowell Colony, PJ Mark, Open City, Greg Purcell, Saïd Sayrafiezadeh, Richard VanFulpen, and Joanna Yas.